SO-CLM-006

RELIGION IN CONTEMPORARY FICTION: CRITICISM FROM 1945 TO THE PRESENT

RELIGION IN CONTEMPORARY FICTION: CRITICISM FROM 1945 TO THE PRESENT

Compiled by

George N. Boyd
and
Lois A. Boyd

TRINITY UNIVERSITY PRESS • SAN ANTONIO, TEXAS

Library of Congress Catalog Card number 73-83689
SBN, #911536-51-5
Printed by Best Printing Company, Inc.
Bound by Custom Bookbinders, Inc.
Copyright 1973 by Trinity University Press
Printed in the United States of America

45,673

Checklists in the Humanities and Education: A Series

Harry B. Caldwell, Trinity University, General Editor

As a continuing effort, *Checklists in the Humanities and Education: A Series* endeavors to provide the student with essential bibliographical information on important scholarly subjects not readily available in composite form. The series emphasizes selection and limitation of both primary and secondary works, providing a practical and convenient research tool as a primary aim. For example, this present compilation of criticism devoted to religious themes and topics in contemporary fiction is confined to English-language criticism of writers belonging to the period following World War II. The inclusion of materials from the more general field of religion and the arts is limited to criticism particularly relevant to the narrower topic. Likewise, subsequent volumes will remain characteristically selective, limited, and concise.

* * * * * *

The general editor wishes to thank Anselm Atkins of Emory University for his careful reading of the manuscript and for his pertinent suggestions; the staffs of the Trinity University Libraries, the University of Texas Libraries in Austin, the Academic Library of St. Mary's University in San Antonio, and the Oblate College of the Southwest Library in San Antonio, for their helpful cooperation; and Sharon Purvis and Patti Bender, students at Trinity University, for their aid in proofreading.

PREFACE

The current revolution in theology's self-understanding, which sets aside the traditional Western subjugation of religion to "right belief" and "right conduct," has had as one of its principal features a burgeoning study of the relation of religion and the arts. At least from the side of religion a more ancient tradition of their intrinsic intertwining is being recovered. That intertwining, heretofore kept feebly alive mostly from the side of the arts, is rooted in religion's and art's common concern to structure and express the quest of the human spirit. Both the religious and the poetic imagination tend to orient man's consciousness internally, socially, and within nature, on the one hand, and to express man's unique and creative potentiality on the other.

Admittedly, some of the critical work on the relation of religion and the arts still reflects primarily illustrative and apologetic interests. Most criticism expressing religious interests, however, recognizes the artist as the creator and articulator of contemporary myth and the celebrator of human creativity, rather than as a gifted diagnostician of a spiritual malaise for which religion can then prescribe the remedy. Moreover, such work is increasingly produced by persons thoroughly trained in literary criticism.

The specialization in contemporary fiction of this bibliography stems partly from the editors' interests and partly from the belief that fiction is the single most common focus of the renewed interest in religion and the arts. The bibliography is intended to be an especially valuable research aid to the undergraduate student and the scholar working only part time in the field.

The first part of the bibliography lists English-language criticism dealing with the relation of theological motifs, themes, and topics to contemporary fiction and with analysis of the influence of religion on the work of selected post-World War II novelists.* The second part lists material from the broader area of religion, literature, and the arts which is important to the understanding of the relation of religion and fiction. Earlier bibliographies in religion and literature are listed in part three.

To make an extensive body of material as workable as possible for the researcher, the essays and books have been divided into descriptive categories. In many instances a piece of material may be listed under more than one category. We have attempted to cross-refer accurately and thoroughly; however, there was inevitably some measure of arbitrariness. Likewise, the categories themselves are not easily assigned, and, when in doubt, we made the choice on the basis of the orientation most prevalent in articles within the heading. The selection of primary authors also involves a measure of subjectivity. Generally the bibliography is oriented to English-language novelists, and translated authors are included only where the religious significance of their work, as reflected in English-language criticism, is prominent. +

We have generally noted multiple sources of a piece of material. However, this bibliography is not intended as an exhaustive compilation. We have not included unpublished dissertations, reviews of novels or critical work, or routine discussions in histories of literature, encyclopedias, and reference works.

We have attempted to bring this compilation as nearly up-to-date as possible by use of all available resources through 1972 and continuing into 1973. The Appendices list materials recorded between compilation and publication. All items in the Appendices are crossrefered into the appropriate subject categories within the body of the checklist.

Wherever possible, studies cited have been examined personally, to check both the accuracy of the entry and the relevance of the material to the general topic.

The forms of the entries are as follows:

Books: 29. Scott, N. A., Jr. *Craters of the Spirit: Studies in the Modern Novel.* Washington-Cleveland: Corpus Books, 1968; London: Sheed & Ward, 1969. This is item 29 and lists author, book title, place and name of publisher and date of publication.

Articles: 6. Detweiler, R. "American Fiction and the Loss of Faith," *ThT*, 21 (1964): 161-173. This is item 6. R. Detweiler is the author,

---

*In selecting writers, we have included several whose productivity began prior to 1945. For coherence, we have listed criticism written since 1945 of both their pre- and post-war work.

+Some authors not dealt with but whose work may be of further or future interest to critics concerned with religious implications of their work might include Jean-Paul Sartre, André Malraux, Aleksandr I. Solzhenitsyn, Günter Grass, Heinrich Böll, Samuel Beckett, Alan Paton, Chaim Potok, Jorge Luis Borges, Nathalie Sarraute, Joyce Carol Oates.

"American Fiction and the Loss of Faith" is the article. It appeared in *Theology Today* (see the list of abbreviations), volume 21, in 1964, and is on pages 161-173. When an issue number is needed, it appears in lower-case roman after the arabic volume number.

If a book or essay is listed several times, the full reference is given only once. Subsequent references are indicated only by a notation: *See 171*, for example, referring to the original listing. When chapters of a book are listed separately, the reference lists author, title, pages and the notation: See item 177 (for example). The item number gives the location of the full reference of the book.

GNB
LAB
San Antonio, Texas
April, 1973

ABBREVIATIONS

Accent	
America	
ABR	*American Benedictine Review*
AI	*American Imago*
AL	*American Literature*
AQ	*American Quarterly*
ASch	*American Scholar*
ANQ	*Andover Newton Quarterly*
ATR	*Anglican Theological Review*
AR	*Antioch Review*
Approach	
ArQ	*Arizona Quarterly*
Atlan	*Atlantic Monthly*
BA	*Books Abroad*
BuR	*Bucknell Review*
BB	*Bulletin of Bibliography*
CQ	*Cambridge Quarterly*
CJT	*Canadian Journal of Theology*
CaSE	*Carnegie Series in English*
CathER	*Catholic Educational Review*
CathM	*Catholic Mind*
CathW	*Catholic World*
CentR	*Centennial Review*
ChiR	*Chicago Review*
ChrC	*Christian Century*

ChrS	Christian Scholar (See also Soundings)
C&C	Christianity and Crisis
CimR	Cimarron Review
Cithara	
CE	College English
CLAJ	College Language Association Journal
ColBQ	College of the Bible Quarterly
ColQ	Colorado Quarterly
CTSB	Columbia Theological Seminary Bulletin
Commentary	
Commonweal	
CL	Comparative Literature
CLS	Comparative Literature Studies
CTM	Concordia Theological Monthly
ConL	Contemporary Literature
ConR	Contemporary Review
Continuum	
Cresset	
Criticism	
Critic	
CritQ	Critical Quarterly
Crit	Critique
CrCur	Cross Currents
Culture	
Daedalus	
DR	Dalhousie Review
Discourse	
DownR	Downside Review
DubR	Dublin Review
Encounter	
EJ	English Journal
English Record	
ELH	Journal of English Literary History
ES	English Studies
EIC	Essays in Criticism
Ethics	
ExpT	Expository Times
ForumH	Forum (Houston)
Foun	Foundations
FourQ	Four Quarters
FR	French Review
FS	French Studies
GeorR	Georgia Review

GL&L	*German Life and Letters*
GR	*Germanic Review*
GOTR	*Greek Orthodox Theological Review*
Greyfriar	
Harper	*Harper's Magazine*
HQ	*Hartford Quarterly*
HTR	*Harvard Theological Review*
HJ	*Hibbert Journal*
HC	*The Hollins Critic*
HR	*Hopkins Review*
IPQ	*International Philosophical Quarterly*
Interpretation	
IEY	*Iowa English Yearbook*
JAAC	*Journal of Aesthetics and Art Criticism*
JAF	*Journal of American Folklore*
JAAR	*Journal of the American Academy of Religion* (Formerly JB&R)
JB&R	*Journal of Bible and Religion* (See also JAAR)
JGE	*Journal of General Education*
JP	*Journal of Philosophy*
Journal of Popular Culture	
JR	*Journal of Religion*
JRT	*Journal of Religious Thought*
Judaism	
KR	*Kenyon Review*
LTQ	*Lexington Theological Quarterly*
Listening	
L&RN	*Literature and Religion Newsletter*
LQ	*Lutheran Quarterly*
MankSE	*Mankato Studies in English*
MR	*Massachusetts Review*
MQ	*Midwest Quarterly*
MinnR	*Minnesota Review*
MissQ	*Mississippi Quarterly*
MFS	*Modern Fiction Studies*
MLJ	*Modern Language Journal*
MLN	*Modern Language Notes*
MLQ	*Modern Language Quarterly*
MLR	*Modern Language Review*
Month	
Nation	
NEQ	*New England Quarterly*

NewBl	*New Blackfriars*
New Repub	*New Republic*
NSch	*New Scholasticism*
NCCL	*Newsletter of the Conference on Christianity and Literature*
NYTBR	*New York Times Book Review*
Novel	
PLL	*Papers on Language and Literature*
ParisR	*Paris Review*
PR	*Partisan Review*
Person	*The Personalist*
Philosophy	
PQ	*Philological Quarterly*
Phylon	
PrS	*Prairie Schooner*
PresbyL	*Presbyterian Life*
PSB	*Princeton Seminary Bulletin*
PMLA	*Publication of the Modern Language Association*
QRLit	*Quarterly Review of Literature*
QQ	*Queen's Quarterly*
RampMag	*Ramparts Magazine*
Reformed Journal	
RIL	*Religion in Life*
RelStudies	*Religious Studies*
RelEd	*Religious Education*
Renascence	
Response	
REL	*Review of English Literature*
R&E	*Review and Expositor*
RevM	*Review of Metaphysics*
RevP	*Review of Politics*
RQ	*Riverside Quarterly*
RusR	*Russian Review*
SatR	*Saturday Review*
SR	*Sewanee Review*
Soundings (formerly *ChrS*)	
SAQ	*South Atlantic Quarterly*
SDR	*South Dakota Review*
SHR	*Southern Humanities Review*
SLJ	*Southern Literary Journal*
SoQ	*The Southern Quarterly*
SoR	*Southern Review* (LSU)
SoWestR	*Southwest Review*
SWJT	*Southwestern Journal of Theology*
Spectator	

Studies: An Irish Quarterly Review	
SLitI	*Studies in the Literary Imagination*
SIP	*Studies in Philology*
SSF	*Studies in Short Fiction*
Symposium	
TamR	*Tamarack Review*
TQ	*Texas Quarterly*
Th	*Theology*
ThT	*Theology Today*
Thought	
TLS	*Times Literary Supplement*
Trace	
Tradition	
TuSE	*Tulane Studies in English*
TC	*Twentieth Century*
TCL	*Twentieth Century Literature*
TCS	*Twentieth Century Studies*
USQR	*Union Seminary Quarterly Review*
Universitas	
UDQ	*University of Denver Quarterly*
UKCR	*University of Kansas City Review* (See *UR*)
UMSE	*University of Mississippi Studies in English*
UPR	*University of Portland Review*
UTQ	*University of Toronto Quarterly*
UR	*University Review* (formerly UKCR)
VQR	*Virginia Quarterly Review*
Western American Literature	
WHR	*Western Humanities Review*
XUS	*Xavier University Studies*
YFS	*Yale French Studies*
YLM	*Yale Literary Magazine*
YR	*Yale Review*
YCGL	*Yearbook of Comparative and General Literature*

TABLE OF CONTENTS

Joseph Heller
Ernest Hemingway
Nikos Kazantzakis
Ken Kesey
Arthur Koestler
Gertrud von LeFort
Carson McCullers
Norman Mailer
Bernard Malamud
François Mauriac
Henry Miller
Vladimir Nabokov
Edwin O'Connor
Flannery O'Connor
George Orwell
Boris Pasternak
Walker Percy
Katherine Anne Porter
J. F. Powers
James Purdy
Thomas Pynchon
Philip Roth
J. D. Salinger
Ignazio Silone
Isaac Bashevis Singer
Muriel Spark
John Steinbeck
William Styron
J. R. R. Tolkien
John Updike
Kurt Vonnegut
Edward Lewis Wallant
Evelyn Waugh
Elie Wiesel
Richard Wright

I. RELIGION IN CONTEMPORARY FICTION

I. RELIGION IN
CONTEMPORARY FICTION

A. General Critical Studies

1. Anderson, D. *The Tragic Protest; a Christian Study of Some Modern Literature.* Richmond, Virginia: John Knox Press, 1969.

2. Atkins, A. "Theology and the Novel," *Response,* 10 (1968-69): 73-79.

3. Brown, R. Mc. "Salinger, Steinbeck and Company: Assyrians in Modern Dress," *PresbyL* (May 1, 1962): 16-17, 32-33.

4. Bunting, J. J., Jr. "Religion Among the Novelists," *RIL,* 24 (1955): 208-218.

5. Cismaru, A. "Religion: A Focal Point in French Literature," *Renascence,* 16 (1963): 42-47.

6. Detweiler, R. "American Fiction and the Loss of Faith," *ThT,* 21 (1964): 161-173.

7. Detweiler, R. "Faith and Fiction in Our Time" *Response,* 10 (1968-69): 51-58.

8. Detweiler, R. *Four Spiritual Crises in Mid-Century American Fiction.* University of Florida Monographs # 14, Fall, 1963. Gainesville, Florida: University of Florida Press, 1964.

9. Forgey, W. "The Novel's Angle of Vision," *ANQ,* 3 (1962): 8-17.

10. Gass, W. H. *Fiction and the Figures of Life.* New York: Knopf, 1970.

11. Gordon, C. "Some Readings and Misreadings," *SR,* 61 (1953): 384-407.

12. Gregory, H. "Mutations of Belief in the Contemporary Novel," in *Spiritual Problems in Contemporary Literature,* ed. by S. R. Hopper, pp. 35-44. See item 755.

13. Harrison, D. "The American Adam and the Canadian Christ," *TCL,* 16 (1970): 161-167.

14. Hassan, I. H. "Way Down and Out: Spiritual Deflection in Recent American Fiction." *VQR,* 39 (1963): 81-93.

15. Isherwood, C. "The Problem of the Religious Novel," in *Exhumations.* London: Methuen and Company Ltd., 1966, pp. 116-120.

16. Killinger, J., Jr. "Three Lost Enormities: Theological Implications of the Modern Novel," *ColBQ,* 38 (1961): 1-15.

17. Kort, W. "Recent Fiction and its Religious Implications," *CLS,* 3 (1966): 223-234.

18. Lewis, R. W. B. "American Letters: A Projection," *YR,* 51 (1961): 211-226. See especially pp. 219-226.

19. Lewis, R. W. B. *The Picaresque Saint: Representative Figures in Contemporary Fiction.* Philadelphia and New York: J. P. Lippincott Company, 1959.

20. Mooney, H. J., Jr. and T. F. Staley. *The Shapeless God: Essays in Modern Fiction.* University of Pittsburgh Press, 1968.

21. Mueller, W. R. *Celebration of Life: Studies in Modern Fiction.* New York: Sheed & Ward, 1972.

22. Mueller, W. R. *The Prophetic Voice in Modern Fiction.* New York: Association Press, 1959.

23. O'Connor, F. *Mystery and Manners,* ed. by S. and R. Fitzgerald. New York: Farrar, Straus & Giroux, 1969.

24. Penick, E. A., Jr. "Voices on the Bridge: Fiction and Theology in Dialogue and Transition," *JR,* 50 (1970): 408-419.

25. Roland, A. "Christian Implications in Anti-Stalinist Novels," *RIL*, 22 (1953): 400-412.

26. Savage, D. S. "Truth and the Art of the Novel," in *The New Orpheus*, ed. by N. A. Scott, Jr., pp. 290-304. See item 856.

27. Scholes, R. *The Fabulators*. New York: Oxford University Press, 1967.

28. Scott, N. A., Jr., ed. *Adversity and Grace*. Chicago: The University of Chicago Press, 1968.

29. Scott, N. A., Jr. *Craters of the Spirit: Studies in the Modern Novel*. Washington-Cleveland: Corpus Books, 1968; London: Sheed & Ward, 1969.

30. Scott, N. A., Jr., ed. *Forms of Extremity in the Modern Novel*. Richmond: John Knox Press, 1965.

31. Slavitt, D. R. "Poetry, Novels and Critics," *YR*, 51 (1962): 502-504.

32. Sullivan, W. "Southern Writers in the Modern World: Death by Melancholy," *SoR*, 6 n.s. (1970): 907-919.

33. Waldmeir, J. J. "Only An Occasional Rutabaga: American Fiction Since 1945," *MFS*, 15 (1969-1970): 467-482.

34. Wilder, A. N. "Strategies of the Christian Artist," *C&C*, 25 (1965): 92-95. Reply by H. H. Rockwell and rejoinder in 25 (1965): 167-168.

35. Winship, G. P., Jr. "Mission to Novelists," *ChrC*, 73 (1956): 75-76.

36. Zylstra, H. *Testament of Vision*. Grand Rapids: Eerdmans, 1958. *See also* 184, 286, 913, 953, 959, 960, 974, 988, 991, 1001, 1021.

B. Criticism Dealing with Theological Motifs and Themes in Fiction

APOCALYPSE

37. Alter, R. "Apocalyptic Temper," *Commentary*, 41 (1966): 61-66.

38. Boklund, G. "Time Must Have a Stop: Apocalyptic Thought and Expression in the Twentieth Century," *UDQ*, 2 (1967): 69-98.

39. Dudley, G., III. "Importance of Being Earnest about Christian Myth," *ChrC*, 84 (1967): 1215-1218.

40. Lewis, R. W. B. "Days of Wrath and Laughter," in *Trials of the Word: Essays in American Literature and the Humanistic Tradition,* pp. 184-235. See item 177.

41. May, J. R. "Images of Apocalypse in the Black Novel," *Renascence,* 23 (1970-71): 31-45.
    See also 835, 943, 1003, 1007, 1011.

CELEBRATION

42. Rupp, R. H. *Celebration in Post-War American Fiction: 1945-1967.* Coral Gables, Florida: University of Miami Press, 1970.
    See also 21, 999.

CHRIST

43. Brumm, U. "Christ and Adam as 'Figures' in American Literature," in *American Thought and Religious Typology,* pp. 198-221. See item 169.

44. Brumm, U. "The Figure of Christ in American Literature," *PR,* 24 (1957): 403-413.

45. Deffner, D. L. "The Christ-Figure in Contemporary Literature," *CTM,* 34 (1963): 278-283.

46. Detweiler, R. "Christ and the Christ Figure in American Fiction," *ChrS,* 47 (1964): 111-124. [Collected in *New Theology No. 2,* ed. by M. E. Marty and D. G. Peerman. New York: Macmillan, 1965, pp. 297-316.]

47. Detweiler, R. "Christ in American Religious Fiction," *JB&R,* 32 (1964): 8-14.

48. Dougherty, C. T. "The Christ-Figure in *The Grapes of Wrath,*" *CE,* 24 (1962): 224-226.

49. Downing, C. "Typology and the Literary Christ-figure; a critique," *JAAR,* 36 (1968): 13-27.

50. Feuerlicht, I. "Christ Figures in Literature," *Person,* 48 (1967): 461-472.

51. Hauck, R. B. "The Comic Christ and the Modern Readers," *CE,* 31 (1970): 498-506.

52. Kritzeck, J. "Christ in a Novel: Through Moslem Eyes," *Commonweal,* 65 (1956): 230-232.

53. Moseley, E. M. *Pseudonyms of Christ in the Modern Novel; Motifs and Methods.* University of Pittsburgh Press, [c. 1962].

54. Paton, A. and L. Pope. "The Novelist and Christ," *SatR*, 37 (December 4, 1954): 15-16, 56-59.

55. Tischler, N. M. "The Christ Archetype in Modern Criticism," *NCCL*, 17, ii (1968): 19-25.
    See also 202, 385, 490, 849, 962.

DEATH

56. Hoffman, F. J. *The Mortal No: Death and the Modern Imagination.* Princeton, New Jersey: Princeton University Press, 1964.

57. Wilder, A. N. "Mortality and Contemporary Literature," *HTR*, 58 (1965): 1-20. [Collected in *The Modern Vision of Death*, ed. by N. A. Scott, Jr. Richmond: John Knox Press, 1967, pp. 17-44.]
    See also 186, 729, 905, 966.

EVIL

58. Amstutz, J. "Sickness and Evil in Modern Literature," *RIL*, 34 (1965): 288-298.

59. Hassan, I. H. "The Victim: Images of Evil in Recent American Fiction," *CE*, 21 (1960): 140-146.

60. Kahn, S. J. "The Problem of Evil in Literature," *JAAC*, 12 (1953): 98-110.

61. Wilson, C. "The Power of Darkness," in *The Strength to Dream*, pp. 128-156. See item 884.
    See also 419, 530, 566, 968, 1002.

FAITH

62. Anonymous. "Faith and the Writer: Christian Dimensions in Literature," *TLS* (October 13, 1961): 696-697.

63. Glicksberg, C. I. "Fiction, Philosophy and Faith," in *Literature and Religion: A Study in Conflict*, pp. 169-180. See item 747.
    See also 6, 7, 163, 297, 462, 709, 851, 854.

FALL

64. DeJong, P. "Camus and Bonhoeffer on the Fall," *CJT*, 7 (1961): 245-257.

65. Dillistone, F. W. "The Fall: Christian Truth and Literary Symbol," *CLS*, 2 (1965): 349-362. [Collected in *Mansions of the Spirit*, ed. by G. A. Panichas, pp. 137-154. See item 770. Also in *Comparative Literature: Matter and Method*, ed. by A. O. Aldridge. Urbana, Chicago, Illinois: University of Illinois Press, 1969, pp. 144-157.]
    See also 189, 276, 303, 347, 360, 388, 965, 974.

GOD

66. Glicksberg, C. I. "The God of Fiction," in *Literature and Religion: A Study in Conflict,* pp. 181-191. See item 747.

67. Killinger, J. "The Absence of God in Modern Literature," in *Religion and Contemporary Western Culture,* ed. by E. Cell. Nashville & New York: Abingdon Press, 1967, pp. 176-185.
    See also 81, 147, 163, 329, 442, 452.

GRACE

68. Boyd, G. N. "Parables of Costly Grace: Flannery O'Connor and Ken Kesey," *ThT,* 29 (1972): 161-171.

69. Hoffman, F. J. *The Mortal No: Death and the Modern Imagination.* Princeton, New Jersey: Princeton University Press, 1964. See especially Part I on Grace: 23-135.

70. Noel, D. C. "Post-Modern Literature and the Idea of Grace," *CrCur,* 20 (1970): 99-102.
    See also 318, 426, 450, 527, 528, 541, 562, 573, 579, 616, 687, 703.

INCARNATION

71. Scott, N. A., Jr. "The Meaning of the Incarnation for Modern Literature," *C&C,* 18 (1958): 173-175.

LOVE

See 186, 313, 453, 498, 627, 638, 740.

RECONCILIATION

See 85, 263.

REDEMPTION

72. Dillistone, F. W. *The Novelist and the Passion Story.* New York: Sheed & Ward, 1960.

73. Schall, J. V. "The Crisis of Redemption in Modern Literature," *RIL,* 33 (1964): 617-630.

74. Shurr, W. "Themes of Redemption in Modern Literature," *CathER,* 61 (1963): 83-106.
    See also 68, 352, 381, 388, 502, 506, 528, 545, 598, 647.

SALVATION

75. Moeller, C. *Man and Salvation in Literature.* Tr. by C. U. Quinn. Notre Dame, London: University of Notre Dame Press, 1970.

76. Padovano, A. T. "Salvation Themes in American Literature," in *American Culture and the Quest for Christ,* by A. T. Padovano. New York: Sheed & Ward, 1970, pp. 162-284.
    See also 427, 531, 554, 957.

SATAN/DEVIL IMAGERY

See 315, 339, 411, 440, 555, 615, 645, 1006.

SIN

77. Mauriac, F. "Literature and Sin," in *Second Thoughts: Reflections on Literature and On Life,* by F. Mauriac. Cleveland and New York: The World Publishing Company, 1961, pp. 34-40.
See also 450, 463, 464, 465, 579.

C. Criticism Relating Selected Topics to Religion in Fiction

THE ABSURD

78. Friedman, M. "The Dialogue with the Absurd: The Later Camus and Franz Kafka; Wiesel and the Modern Job," in *To Deny Our Nothingness,* pp. 335-354. See item 210.

79. Galloway, D. D. *The Absurd Hero in American Fiction: Updike, Styron, Bellow and Salinger,* revised edition. Austin: University of Texas Press, 1970.

80. Glicksberg, C. I. "The Literature of Absurdity," in *Literature and Religion: A Study in Conflict,* pp. 200-211. See item 747.

81. Killinger, J. "Camus and After: God in the Literature of Absurdity," *LTQ,* 5 (1970) : 85-110.

82. Miller, J. E. *Quests Surd and Absurd.* Chicago: University of Chicago Press, 1967. See especially Part I, chapter 1, "The Quest Absurd: The New American Novel," pp. 3-30.
See also 147, 163, 337, 340, 341, 935, 986.

ALIENATION

83. Bloomfield, C. "Religion and Alienation in James Baldwin, Bernard Malamud, and James F. Powers," *RelEd,* 57 (1962) : 97-102, 158.

84. Finklestein, S. *Existentialism and Alienation in American Literature.* New York: International Publishers, 1965.

85. Scott, N. A., Jr. *Rehearsals of Discomposure: Alienation and Reconciliation in Modern Literature.* New York: King's Crown Press of Columbia University, 1952 [first printing]; 1958 [second printing].
See also 290, 858.

ALLEGORY

86. Scholes, R. "Fabulation and Allegory," in *The Fabulators*, pp. 97-132. See item 27.
    See also 306, 559, 673, 704.

BELIEF AND THE WRITER

87. Abrams, M. H. "Belief and Disbelief," *UTQ*, 27 (1958): 117-136.

88. Abrams, M. H., ed. *Literature and Belief*. New York: Columbia University Press, 1958.

89. Daiches, D. "Literature and Belief," in *A Study of Literature for Readers and Critics*. Cornell University Press, 1948, pp. 212-226.

90. Enright, D. J. "Literature And/Or Belief: A Progress Report," *EIC*, 6 (1956): 60-69.

91. Hasley, L. "The Interpretation of Beliefs in Literature," *CLAJ*, 5 (1961): 95-105.

92. O'Connor, F. "Novelist and Believer," in *Mystery and Manners*, pp. 154-168. See item 23.

93. Ong, W. J. "Voice as Summons for Belief: Literature, Faith, and the Divided Self," in *Literature and Religion*, ed. by G. B. Gunn, pp. 68-86. See item 750.

94. Savage, D. S. "Truth and the Art of the Novel," in *The New Orpheus*, ed. by N. A. Scott, Jr., pp. 290-304. See item 856.

95. Turnell, M. "Belief and the Writer," *Commonweal*, 62 (1955): 143-146. Reply by C. Jessey, 62 (1955): 257. Rejoinder, 62 (1955): 331-332.
    See also 12, 19, 34, 62, 171, 274, 299, 702, 812, 836, 851, 854, 874.

THE BIBLE

96. Baker, C. "The Place of the Bible in American Fiction," *ThT*, 17 (1960): 53-76.

97. Wilder, A. "Biblical Genres and Archetypes," in *The New Voice*, pp. 41-122. See item 789.
    See also 630, 668, 952, 982.

BLACK FICTION

98. Grumbach, D. "Christianity and Black Writers," *Renascence*, 23 (1970-71): 198-212.

99. Hyman, S. E. "American Negro Literature and the Folk Tradition," in *The Promised End*. Cleveland and New York: World Pub-

lishing Company, 1963, pp. 295-315. See especially pp. 310-312.

100. Killinger, J. "The Black Man and the White God," *RIL,* 39 (1970) : 498-521.

101. Scott, N. A., Jr. "Judgment Marked by a Cellar: The American Negro Writer and the Dialectic of Despair," *UDQ,* 2 (1967) : 5-35. [Collected in *The Shapeless God,* ed. by H. J. Mooney and T. Staley, pp. 139-169. See item 20.]

102. Tischler, N. P. "Negro Novels and Christian Readers," *NCCL,* 21 (1971-72) : 36-41.
See also 41, 301, 305.

BUDDHISM

103. Antico, J. "Parody of J. D. Salinger: Esmé and the Fat Lady Exposed," *MFS,* 12 (1966) : 325-340.

104. Ashida, M. E. "Frogs and Frozen Zen," *PrS,* 34 (1960) : 199-206.

105. Goldstein, B. and S. "Zen and Salinger," *MFS,* 12 (1966) : 313-324.
See also 984.

CALVINISM

106. Boies, J. J. "The Calvinist Obsession in American Letters," *JGE,* 19 (1964) : 57-70.

107. Boulger, J. D. "Puritan Allegory in Four Modern Novels," *Thought,* 44 (1969) : 413-432.
See also 374, 387, 405.

CATHOLICISM

108. Braybrooke, N. "Catholics and the Novel," *Renascence,* 5 (1952) : 22-32.

109. Curley, T. F. "Catholic Novels and American Culture," *Commentary,* 36 (1963) : 34-42.

110. Fowlie, W. "Catholic Orientation in Contemporary French Literature," in *Spiritual Problems in Contemporary Literature,* by S. R. Hopper, pp. 225-242. See item 755.

111. Friedman, M. J. *The Vision Obscured[:] Perceptions of Some Twentieth-Century Catholic Novelists.* New York: Fordham University Press, 1970.

112. Gardiner, H. C. "A New Direction for Creative Writing," *CathM,* 55 (1957) : 526-529. [Originally appeared in *Books on Trial* (April-May, 1957).]

113. Green, M. B. *Yeats's Blessings on von Hügel: Essays on Literature and Religion.* New York: Norton [c. 1967].

114. Hatzfield, H. "Comparison of the Creative and Critical Achievements of the Catholic Revival in France and Germany," *PMLA,* 75 (1960) : 293-296.

115. Hebblethwaite, P. "How Catholic is the Catholic Novel?", *TLS,* 3 (July 27, 1967) : 678-679.

116. Jackson, M. "Jonas and the Whale: On Catholic Writing," *DubR,* 231 (1957) : 334-342.

117. Kellogg, G. "The Catholic Novel in Convergence," *Thought,* 45 (1970) : 265-296.

118. Kellogg, G. *The Vital Tradition[:] The Catholic Novel in a Period of Convergence.* Chicago: Loyola University Press, 1970. [Deals with Greene, Waugh, F. O'Connor, Mauriac, Bernanos, Powers.]

119. Marshall, B. "The Responsibilities of the Catholic Novelist," *Commonweal,* 50 (1949) : 169-171.

120. Mauriac, F. "The Catholic Writer," in *Cain, Where Is Your Brother?* by F. Mauriac. New York: Coward-McCann, Inc., 1962, pp. 149-156.

121. Novak, M. "The Catholic as Writer: II. Prophecy and the Novel," *Commonweal,* 77 (1963) : 563-569.

122. O'Connor, F. "The Catholic Novelist in the Protestant South," in *Mystery and Manners,* pp. 191-212. See item 23.

123. O'Connor, F. "Catholic Novelists and Their Readers," in *Mystery and Manners,* pp. 169-190. See item 23.

124. O'Connor, F. "The Church and the Fiction Writer," *America,* 96 (1957) : 733-735. [Collected in *Mystery and Manners,* by F. O'Connor, pp. 143-153. See item 23.]

125. O'Connor, F. "The Role of the Catholic Novelist," *Greyfriar,* 7 (1964) : 512.

126. Rago, H. "Catholicism in America: Catholics in Literature," *Commonweal,* 59 (1953) : 81-84.

127. Sheed, W. "The Catholic as Writer: I. Enemies of Catholic Promise," *Commonweal,* 77 (1963) : 560-563.

128. Sonnenfeld, A. "The Catholic Novelist and the Supernatural," *FS,* 22 (1968) : 307-319.

129. Sonnenfeld, A. "Twentieth Century Gothic: Reflections on the Catholic Novel," *SoR*, 1 n.s. (1965): 388-405.

130. Sylvester, H. "Problems of the Catholic Writer," *Atlan*, 181 (1948): 109-113.
     See also 134, 178, 285, 288, 292, 441, 791, 839, 863.

CLERGY

131. Davies, H. *A Mirror of the Ministry in Modern Novels.* New York: Oxford University Press, 1959.

132. Garriott, C. T. "The Minister in Recent Fiction," *ChrC*, 65 (1948): 732-733.

133. Hurley, N. P. "The Priest in Literature," *America*, 102 (1960): 496-498.

134. Kunkel, F. L. "Priest as Scapegoat in the Modern Catholic Novel," *RampMag*, 1 (1962): 72-78.

135. Lynn, R. W. "The New Literary Hero," *RIL*, 19 (1950): 255-263.

136. Sandra, Sister M. "The Priest-Hero in Modern Fiction," *Person*, 46 (1965): 527-542.
     See also 524, 608.

COMEDY

137. D'Arcy, M. C. "Literature as a Christian Comedy." *The McAuley Lectures*, 1961. West Hartford, Connecticut: St. Joseph College, 1962, pp. 49-65.

138. Hyers, M. C., ed. *Holy Laughter[:] Essays on Religion in the Comic Perspective.* New York: Seabury Press, 1969.

139. Lynch, W. F. "Theology and the Imagination III: The Problem of Comedy," *Thought*, 30 (1955): 18-36.

140. Mueller, W. R. "God's Fools: Biblical and Modern," *ThT*, 23 (1967): 538-550.

141. Scott, N. A., Jr. "The Bias of Comedy and the Narrow Escape into Faith," *ChrS*, 44 (1961): 9-39. [Collected in *Comedy: Meaning and Form*, ed. by R. W. Corrigan. San Francisco: Chandler Publishing Company, 1965, pp. 81-115. Also in *Holy Laughter*, ed. by M. C. Hyers, pp. 45-74. See item 138.]

142. Shumaker, W. "Tragedy and Comedy," in *Literature and the Irrational*, pp. 157-200. See item 781.

143. Ulanov, B. "The Rhetoric of Christian Comedy," *The McAuley Lectures*, 1961. West Hartford, Conn.: St. Joseph College, 1962, pp. 67-80. [Collected in *Holy Laughter*, ed. by M. C. Hyers, pp. 103-122. See item 138.]

144.   Vos, N. *For God's Sake Laugh.* Richmond: John Knox Press, 1967.
See also 51, 423, 469, 923, 924, 1024.

THE DEATH OF GOD

145.   Detweiler, R. "Poetics and the Death of God," *RIL,* 36 (1967): 270-289.

146.   Glicksberg, C. I. "Eros and the Death of God," *WHR,* 13 (1959): 357-368.

147.   Glicksberg, C. I. "The God of Fiction," *ColQ,* 7 (1958): 207-220.

148.   Glicksberg, C. I. *Modern Literature and the Death of God.* The Hague: Martinus Nijhoff, 1966.

149.   Killinger, J. "The Death of God in American Literature," *SHR,* 2 (1968): 149-172.
See also 701.

DESPAIR

150.   Murchland, B. G. "The Literature of Despair," *Commonweal,* 67 (1958): 527-530.

151.   "Religion and Esthetic Values," *Commonweal,* 71 (1959): 155-167. See especially "The Literature of Despair."
See also 101, 683.

DETECTIVE FICTION

152.   Boyd, A. S. "James Bond: Modern-day Dragonslayer," *ChrC,* 82 (1965): 644-647.

153.   Paul, R. S. "Theology and Detective Fiction," [reprint], *HQ,* 6 (1966): 21-29.

EXISTENTIALISM

154.   Champigny, R. "Existentialism and the Modern French Novel," *Thought,* 31 (1956): 365-384.

155.   Finklestein, S. *Existentialism and Alienation in American Literature.* See item 84.

156.   Glicksberg, C. I. "Existentialism and the Tragic Vision," in *The Tragic Vision in Twentieth-Century Literature,* pp. 97-109. See item 266.

157.   Glicksberg, C. I. "Existentialism in Extremis," *UKCR (UR),* 27 (1960): 31-36.

158.   Glicksberg, C. I. "Literary Existentialism," in *Literature and Religion: A Study in Conflict,* pp. 192-199. See item 747.

159. Hopper, S. R. "Literature—The Author in Search of His Anecdote," in *Restless Adventure: Essays on Contemporary Expressions of Existentialism*, ed. by R. L. Shinn. New York: Scribner, 1968, pp. 90-148.

160. Kern, E. G. *Existential Thought and Fictional Technique: Kierkegaard, Sartre, Beckett*. New Haven: Yale University Press, 1970.

161. Killinger, J. *Hemingway and the Dead Gods: A Study in Existentialism*. Lexington: University of Kentucky Press, 1960.

162. Lehan, R. "Existentialism in Recent American Fiction: The Demonic Quest," *TSLL*, 1 (1959): 181-202.

163. Padovano, A. T. *The Estranged God; Modern Man's Search for Belief*. New York: Sheed & Ward, 1966.

164. Scott, N. A., Jr. *The Unquiet Vision: Mirrors of Man in Existentialism*. New York: The World Publishing Company, 1969.

165. Wilson, C. "The Existential Temper of the Modern Novel," in *Christian Faith and the Contemporary Arts*, ed. by F. Eversole, pp. 115-120. See item 800.
    See also 332, 654, 840, 872, 990.

FANTASY

166. Pitt, V. "Dream and Nightmare," in *The Writer and the Modern World*, pp. 46-72. See item 772.

167. Reilly, R. J. *Romantic Religion[:] A Study of Barfield, Lewis, Williams and Tolkien*. Athens: University of Georgia Press, 1970.

168. Urang, G. *Shadows of Heaven: Religion and Fantasy in the Writing of C. S. Lewis, Charles Williams, and J. R. R. Tolkien*. Philadelphia: Pilgrim Press, 1971.
    See also 167, 507, 691, 693.

HISTORICAL SURVEYS

169. Brumm, U. *American Thought and Religious Typology*, trans. by J. Hooglund. New Brunswick: Rutgers University Press, 1970.

170. Gardiner, H. C., ed. *Fifty Years of the American Novel: A Christian Appraisal*. New York: Gordian Press, Inc., 1968. First printed, Scribner, 1951.

171. Jones, H. M. *Belief and Disbelief in American Literature*. Chicago: University of Chicago Press, 1967.

172. Lewis, R. W. B. *The American Adam[:] Innocence, Tragedy and Tradition in the Nineteenth Century*. Chicago and London: The University of Chicago Press, 1955.

173. MacIver, R. M. *Great Moral Dilemmas in Literature, Past and Present.* New York: Cooper Square Publishers, Inc., 1964.

174. Murdock, K. B. *Literature and Theology in Colonial New England.* Cambridge: Harvard University Press, 1949.

175. Sutcliffe, D. "Christian Themes in American Fiction," *ChrS,* 44 (1961): 297-311.
    See also 188.

HUMANISM

176. Adams, H. B. "Dialogue Between Theology and Modern Humanists: The Contribution of Albert Camus," *Encounter,* 26 (1965): 434-444.

177. Lewis, R. W. B. *Trials of the Word: Essays in American Literature and the Humanistic Tradition.* New Haven and London: Yale University Press, 1965.

178. McLuhan, H. M. "Catholic Humanism and Modern Letters." *The McAuley Lectures,* 1954. West Hartford, Conn.: St. Joseph College, pp. 49-67.

179. Sherrell, R. E. "Theology and Art—A Concern," in *The Human Image: Avant-Garde and Christian.* Richmond: John Knox Press, 1969, pp. 11-30. See especially pp. 19-23.

180. Ulanov, B. *Sources and Resources: The Literary Traditions of Christian Humanism.* Westminster, Maryland: The Newman Press, 1960.
    See also 860, 909, 935.

IDENTITY AND SELF-KNOWLEDGE

181. Glicksberg, C. I. "The Literary Struggle for Selfhood," *Person,* 42 (1961): 52-65.

182. Hoffman, F. J. *The Mortal No: Death and the Modern Imagination.* Princeton, New Jersey: Princeton University Press, 1964. See especially Part III on the Self: 317-493.

183. Jones, W. P. "Self-identity and Contemporary Literature," *ThT,* 19 (1962): 224-234, 255-258.

184. Scott, N. A., Jr. "Society and Self in Recent American Literature," *USQR,* 18 (1963): 377-392. [Collected in *The Search for Identity: Essays on the American Character,* ed. by R. L. Shinn. New York, Institute for Religious and Social Studies; distributed by Harper & Row, 1964, pp. 99-118.]
    See also 215, 313, 914.

IMAGERY

See 350, 534, 568, 580, 707, 744.

INNOCENCE: NEW WORLD MAN

185. Carpenter, F. I. " 'The American Myth': Paradise (To Be) Regained," *PMLA*, 74 (1959): 599-606.

186. Fiedler, L. A. *Love and Death in the American Novel*. New York: Criterion Books, 1960.

187. Milton, J. R. "The American Novel: The Search for Home, Tradition, and Identity," *WHR*, 16 (1962): 169-180.

188. Noble, D. W. *The Eternal Adam and the New World Garden: The Central Myth in the American Novel Since 1830*. New York: Braziller, 1968.

189. Simpson, L. P. "Isaac McCaslin and Temple Drake[:] The Fall of New World Man," in *Nine Essays in Modern Literature*, ed. by D. E. Stanford. Baton Rouge: LSU Press, 1965, pp. 88-106. *See also* 13, 43, 172, 214, 386.

JUDAISM

190. Alter, R. *After the Tradition; Essays on Modern Jewish Writing*. New York: Dutton, 1969.

191. Borowitz, E. B. "Believing Jews and Jewish Writers; Is Dialogue Possible?", *Judaism*, 14 (1965): 172-186.

192. Cargas, H. J. "Holocaust Literature: Today's Burning Bush," *America*, 125 (1971): 458-459.

193. Fiedler, L. "The Jew as Mythic American," *RampMag*, II (Fall 1962): 32-48.

194. Fisch, H. *The Dual Image: The Figure of the Jew in English and American Literature*. New York: Ktav, 1971.

195. Freedman, W. "American Jewish Fiction: So What's the Big Deal?", *ChiR*, 19, i (1966): 90-107.

196. Geismar, M. "The Jewish Heritage in Contemporary American Fiction," *RampMag*, II (Fall 1962): 5-13.

197. Goldin, J. "The Contemporary Jew and His Judaism," in *Spiritual Problems in Contemporary Literature*, ed. by S. R. Hopper, pp. 207-224. See item 755.

198. Guttmann, A. "Conversions of the Jews," *ConL*, 6 (1965): 161-176.

199. Guttmann, A. "Jewish Radicals, Jewish Writers," *ASch,* 32 (1963): 563-575.

200. Malin, I. *Jews and Americans.* Carbondale and Edwardsville: Southern Illinois University Press, 1965.

201. Patterson, D. "The Mishnah and the Novel," *Judaism,* 7 (1958): 337-344.

202. Pinsker, S. "Christ with a Skull Cap: Mixed Metaphors in the American Jewish Novel," *NCCL,* 17, ii (1968): 12-18.

203. Ribalow, H. U. "American Jewish Writers and their Judaism," *Judaism,* 3 (1954): 418-426.

204. Shapiro, K. "The Jewish Writer in America," in *The American Judaism Reader,* ed. by P. Kresh. London, New York, Toronto: Abelard-Schuman, 1967, pp 279-287.

205. Wisse, R. R. *The Schlemiel as Modern Hero.* Chicago: University of Chicago Press, 1971.
     See also 314, 912, 949.

MAN

206. Deffner, D. L. "Paperback in the Pew: Portraits of Man in Modern Literature," *CTM,* 32 (1961): 453-465.

207. Deffner, D. L. "Portraits of Man in Modern Literature," *Universitas,* I (1963): 20-29.

208. Fitch, R. E. "Secular Images of Man in Contemporary Literature," *RelEd,* 53 (1958): 83-91.

209. Friedman, M. *Problematic Rebel,* revised edition. Chicago and London: University of Chicago Press, 1970.

210. Friedman, M. *To Deny Our Nothingness: Contemporary Images of Man.* London: Victor Gollancz Ltd., 1967.

211. Fuller, E. *Man in Modern Fiction: Some Minority Opinions on Contemporary American Writing.* New York: Random House [c. 1958].

212. Hardy, J. E. *Man in the Modern Novel.* Seattle: University of Washington Press, 1964.

213. Hartt, J. N. *The Lost Image of Man.* Baton Rouge, Louisiana: Louisiana State University Press, 1963.

214. Hassan, I. *Radical Innocence: Studies in the Contemporary American Novel.* Princeton: Princeton University Press, 1961.

215. Killinger, J. "The Journey into Self," in *The Failure of Theology in Modern Literature,* pp. 59-83. See item 760.

216. Moeller, C. "The Image of Man in Modern European Literature," in *The New Orpheus,* ed. by N. A. Scott, Jr., pp. 396-406. See item 856.

217. Sherrell, R. E. "Theology and Art—A Concern," in *The Human Image: Avant-Garde and Christian.* Richmond: John Knox Press, 1969, pp. 11-30.

218. Stewart, R. "A Doctrine of Man," *MissQ,* 12 (1959) : 4-9.

219. Stewart, R. "Doctrines of Man in American Literature," *RelEd,* 56 (1961) : 83-89.
See also 75, 164, 243, 407, 410, 415, 831, 999, 1020.

MORALITY

220. Arnold, W. E., Jr. and R. Horchler. "An Exchange of Views: III. Literature and Morality," *Commonweal,* 70 (1960) : 106-107.

221. Canavan, F., G. Carey and R. Horchler. "An Exchange of Views: I Literature and Morality," *Commonweal* 70 (1960) : 54-56.

222. Horchler, R. "Literature and Morality," *Commonweal,* 69 (1959) : 559-561.

223. Hyman, L. W. "Moral Values and the Literary Experience," *JAAC,* 24 (1965-66) : 539-547.

224. Mollenkott, V. *Adamant and Stone Chips.* Waco: Word Books, 1967.

225. "Religion and Esthetic Values," *Commonweal,* 71 (1959) : 155-167. See "Literature and Morality."

226. Wimsatt, W. K., Jr. "Poetry and Morals: A Relation Reargued," in *The New Orpheus,* ed. by N. A. Scott, Jr., pp. 236-252. See item 856.
See also 173, 820.

MYTH

227. Brooks, C. "Christianity, Myth and the Symbolism of Poetry," in *Christian Faith and the Contemporary Arts,* ed. by F. Eversole, pp. 100-107. See item 800.

228. Ellmann, R. and C. Feidelson, Jr. *The Modern Tradition[:] Backgrounds of Modern Literature.* New York: Oxford University Press, 1965. See especially part 6, "Myth," pp. 617-681.

229. Frye, N. "New Directions from Old," in *Myth and Mythmaking,* ed. by H. A. Murray. Boston: Beacon Press, 1968, pp. 115-131. First printed, Braziller, 1960.

230. Shumaker, W. "Myth" in *Literature and the Irrational*, pp. 109-156. See item 781.
   See also 39, 188, 256, 276, 306, 375, 427, 493, 525, 766, 789, 829, 861, 964, 975, 977, 978, 1002, 1029.

NIHILISM

231. Elliott, G. P. "Never Nothing," *Harper*, 241 (September 1970): 83-93.

232. Glicksberg, C. I. "The Aesthetics of Nihilism," *UKCR (UR)*, 27 (1960): 127-130.

233. Glicksberg, C. I. "Nihilism and Tragedy," in *The Tragic Vision in Twentieth-Century Literature*, pp. 3-74. See item 266.
   See also 181, 530, 968.

POPULAR RELIGIOUS FICTION

234. Bode, C. "Lloyd Douglas and America's Largest Parish," *RIL*, 19 (1950): 440-447.

235. Hart, J. D. "Platitudes of Piety: Religion and the Popular Modern Novel," *AQ*, 6 (1954): 311-322.

236. Thorpe, W. "The Religious Novel as Best Seller in America," in *Religious Perspectives in American Culture*, ed. by J. W. Smith and A. L. Jamison. Princeton University Press, 1961, pp. 195-242.

REALITY

237. Elmen, P. "Twice-Blessed Enamel Flowers: Reality in Contemporary Fiction," in *The Climate of Faith in Modern Literature*, ed. by N. A. Scott, Jr., pp. 84-101. See item 851.

238. Wilson, C. "The Implications of Realism" (pp. 30-71) and "'Illusion' and 'Reality'" (pp. 197-201) in *The Strength to Dream*. See item 884.
   See also 256, 258, 658, 735.

RITUAL

239. Moseley, E. M. "Religion and the Literary Genres," *CLS*, 2 (1965): 335-348. [Collected in *Mansions of the Spirit*, ed. by G. A. Panichas, pp. 87-104. See item 770. Also in *Comparative Literature: Matter and Method*, ed. by A. O. Aldridge, pp. 161-174. See item 65.]
   See also 575.

SATIRE

240. Gable, Sister M. "Prose Satire and the Modern Christian Temper," *ABR*, 11 (1960): 21-34.

241. Scholes, R. "Fabulation and Satire," in *The Fabulators,* pp. 35-55. See item 27.

242. Wagoner, W. D. "Bittersweet Grace: Religious Satire," *ThT,* 24 (1967): 44-51.
     See also 604, 628.

SCIENCE FICTION

243. Lantero, E. H. "What Is Man? Theological Aspects of Contemporary Science Fiction," *RIL,* 38 (1969): 242-255.

244. Lantero, E. H. "What Is Time? More Theological Aspects of Science Fiction," *RIL,* 40 (1971): 423-435.

245. Rose, L. and S. *The Shattered Ring.* Richmond: John Knox Press, 1970.
     See also 901, 906, 1008.

SYMBOLISM

246. Ellmann, R. and C. Feidelson, Jr. *The Modern Tradition[:] Backgrounds of Modern Literature.* New York: Oxford University Press, 1965. See especially part 1, "Symbolism," pp. 7-225.

247. Flood, E. "Christian Language in Modern Literature," *Culture,* 22 (March 1961): 28-42.

248. Johnson, F. E., ed. *Religious Symbolism.* New York: Harper, 1955.

249. Kahler, E. "The Nature of the Symbol," in *Symbolism in Religion and Literature,* ed. by R. May, pp. 50-74. See item 252.

250. Lynch, W. F. "Theology and the Imagination II: The Evocative Symbol," *Thought,* 29 (1954): 529-554.

251. May, R. "The Significance of Symbols," in *Symbolism in Religion and Literature,* ed. by R. May, pp. 11-49. See item 252.

252. May, R. ed. *Symbolism in Religion and Literature.* New York: G. Braziller [c. 1960].

253. Moloney, M. F. "Symbolism in Modern Literature," *America,* 92 (1954): 300-302.

254. Tillich, P. "The Religious Symbol," in *Symbolism and Religion,* ed. by R. May, pp. 75-98. See item 252.

255. Wheelwright, P. E. *The Burning Fountain: A Study in the Language of Symbolism,* revised edition. Bloomington & London: Indiana University Press, 1968.

256. Wheelwright, P. *Metaphor and Reality*. Bloomington: Indiana University Press, 1962. [Chapters on symbolism, 92-128; myth, 129-152; reality, 153-173.]

257. Wilder, A. N. "Social Symbolism and the Communication of the Gospel," *C&C*, 20 (1960): 180-182.
      See also 227, 379, 534, 580, 594, 600, 637, 674, 744, 794, 829, 831.

TIME

258. Church, M. *Time and Reality: Studies in Contemporary Fiction*. Chapel Hill: University of North Carolina Press, 1963.

259. Meyerhoff, H. *Time in Literature*. Berkeley and Los Angeles: University of California Press, 1955.

260. Moloney, M. F. "Time and François Mauriac," *Blackfriars* (April 1957): 173-177.

261. Noon, W. T. "Modern Literature and the Sense of Time," *Thought*, 33 (1958-59): 571-603.
      See also 56, 244, 422, 735, 765.

TRAGEDY

262. Cox, R. L. "Tragedy and the Gospel Narratives," *YR*, 57 (1968): 545-570.

263. Driver, T. F. "The Cost of Reconciliation," *USQR*, 13 (1958): 13-17.

264. Gardner, H. "Religion and Tragedy," in *Religion and Literature*, pp. 13-118. See item 746.

265. Glencross, A. F. "Christian Tragedy," *DownR*, 74, no. 232 (1956): 228-233.

266. Glicksberg, C. I. *The Tragic Vision in Twentieth-Century Literature*. Carbondale: Southern Illinois University Press, 1963.

267. Harper, R. "The Dark Night of Sisyphus," in *The Climate of Faith in Modern Literature*, ed. by N. A. Scott, Jr., pp. 65-83. See item 851.

268. Jarrett-Kerr, M. "The Conditions of Tragedy," *CLS*, 2 (1965): 363-374. [Collected in *Mansions of the Spirit*, ed. by G. A. Panichas, pp. 121-136. See item 770.]

269. Jaspers, K. "The Tragic: Awareness, Basic Characteristics, Fundamental Interpretations," in *Tragedy: Modern Essays in Criticism*, ed. by L. Michel and R. B. Sewall. Englewood Cliffs, N.J.: Prentice-Hall, Inc., 1963, pp. 6-26.

270. Kaufmann, W. *Tragedy and Philosophy*. Garden City, N.Y.: Doubleday & Company, Inc., 1968.

271. Krieger, M. *The Tragic Vision: Variations on a Theme in Literary Interpretation.* Chicago & London: The University of Chicago Press [Phoenix books], 1966. Originally published by Holt, Rinehart & Winston, Inc., 1960.

272. Michel, L. "The Possibility of a Christian Tragedy," *Thought,* 31 (1956): 403-428. [Collected in *Tragedy: Modern Essays in Criticism,* ed. by Michel, L. and R. B. Sewall. Englewood Cliffs, N.J.: Prentice-Hall, Inc., 1963, pp. 210-233.]

273. Raphael, D. D. *The Paradox of Tragedy.* Bloomington, Ind.: Indiana University Press, 1960. See especially chapter 2, "Tragedy and Religion": 37-68.

274. Scott, N. A., Jr. *The Tragic Vision and the Christian Faith.* New York: Association Press, 1957.

275. Sewall, R. B. *The Vision of Tragedy.* New Haven: Yale University Press, 1959. See especially chapter 1, "The Vision of Tragedy," chapter 4, "The Tragic Form," and chapter 5, "Tragedy and Christianity."

276. Weisinger, H. *Tragedy and the Paradox of the Fortunate Fall.* East Lansing: Michigan State College Press, 1953. *See also* 142, 456, 686, 794, 860, 970.

VIOLENCE

277. Glicksberg, C. I. "Malraux and the Myth of Violence," in *The Tragic Vision in Twentieth-Century Literature,* pp. 137-147. See item 266.

278. Gossett, L. Y. *Violence in Recent Southern Fiction.* Durham, N.C.: Duke University Press, 1965.

279. Hoffman, F. J. *The Mortal No: Death and the Modern Imagination.* Princeton, New Jersey: Princeton University Press, 1964. See especially Part II on Violence: 139-190. *See also* 573, 575.

D. Criticism Concerned with the Relation of Religion to the Work of Selected Contemporary Authors

GENERAL AND COMPARATIVE

280. Axthelm, P. M. "The Search for a Reconstructed Order: Koestler and Golding," in *The Modern Confessional Novel,* by P. M.

Axthelm. New Haven & London: Yale University Press, 1967, pp. 97-127.

281. Barnes, R. J. "Two Modes of Fiction: Hemingway and Greene," *Renascence,* 14 (1962): 193-198.

282. Baumbach, J. *The Landscape of Nightmare: Studies in the Contemporary American Novel.* New York University Press, 1965.

283. Bradbury, J. M. "Absurd Insurrection: the Barth-Percy Affair," *SAQ,* 68 (1969): 319-329.

284. Brooks, C. *The Hidden God: Studies in Hemingway, Faulkner, Yeats, Eliot and Warren.* New Haven: Yale University Press, 1963.

285. Cameron, J. M. "The Catholic Novelist and European Culture," *TCS,* #1 (1969): 79-94. [Deals with Bernanos, Mauriac, Waugh, and Greene.]

286. Harper, H. M., Jr. *Desperate Faith—a study of Bellow, Salinger, Mailer, Baldwin and Updike.* Chapel Hill: University of North Carolina Press, 1967.

287. Hoffman, F. J. *The Imagination's New Beginning: Theology and Modern Literature.* Notre Dame & London: University of Notre Dame Press, 1967.

288. Jacobsen, J. "A Catholic Quartet," *ChrS,* 47 (1964): 139-154.

289. Kearns, F. E. "Salinger and Golding: Conflict on the Campus," *America,* 108 (1963): 136-139.

290. Klein, M. *After Alienation[:] American Novels in Mid-Century.* Cleveland and New York: World Publishing Company, c. 1962.

291. Kort, W. A. *Shriven Selves: Religious Problems in Recent American Fiction.* Philadelphia: Fortress Press, 1972.

292. O'Donnell, Donat. *Maria Cross[:] Imaginative Patterns in a Group of Modern Catholic Writers.* New York: Oxford University Press, 1952. [Deals with Mauriac, Bernanos, Greene, Waugh.]

293. O'Faolain, S. *The Vanishing Hero.* Boston & Toronto: Atlantic-Little, Brown, 1956.

294. Quinn, Sister M. B. "View from a Rock: The Fiction of Flannery O'Connor and J. F. Powers," *Crit,* 2, ii (1958): 19-27.

295. Reinhardt, K. F. *The Theological Novel of Modern Europe; an Analysis of Masterpieces by Eight Authors.* New York: Ungar Publishing Company, 1969.

296. Stewart, D. *The Ark of God: Studies in Five Modern Novelists.* London: Carey Kingsgate Press Ltd., 1961.

297. Stratford, P. *Faith and Fiction: Creative Process in Greene and Mauriac.* Notre Dame, Ind.: University of Notre Dame Press, 1964.

298. Swanson, W. J. "William Faulkner and William Styron: Notes on Religion," *CimR,* 7 (1969): 45-52.

299. Turnell, M. *Modern Literature and Christian Faith.* Westminster, Maryland: The Newman Press, 1961. See especially chapter III, "Problems of Belief: Claudel-Mauriac-Greene," pp. 49-69.

300. Turnell, M. "The Religious Novel," *Commonweal,* 55 (1951): 55-57.
    See also 961.

JAMES BALDWIN

301. Bone, R. "The Novels of James Baldwin," in *The Black Novelist,* ed. by R. Hemenway. Columbus, Ohio: Charles E. Merrill Publishing Company, 1970, pp. 113-133.

302. Finn, J. "James Baldwin's Vision," *Commonweal,* 78 (1963): 447-449.

303. Foster, D. E. " 'Cause my house fell down': The Theme of the Fall in Baldwin's Novels," *Crit,* 13, ii (1971): 50-62.

304. MacInnes, C. "Dark Angel: The Writings of James Baldwin," *Encounter,* 21, ii (1963): 22-33.

305. Margolies, E. "The Negro Church: James Baldwin and the Christian Vision," in *Native Sons,* by E. Margolies. Philadelphia and New York: J. B. Lippincott Company, 1968, pp. 102-126.
    See also 83, 286, 290.

JOHN BARTH

306. Scholes, R. "Fabulation and Epic Vision," in *The Fabulators,* pp. 135-173. See item 27.

307. Tilton, J. W. "Giles Goat-Boy: An Interpretation," *BuR,* 18 (1970): 92-119.
    See also 177, 283, 1001.

SAUL BELLOW

308. Beebe, H. K. "Biblical Adventures in an American Novel," *JB&R,* 27 (1959): 133-138.

309. Bellow, S. "Deep Readers of the World, Beware!", *NYTBR,* February 15, 1959: 1, 34.

310. Capon, R. F. "Herzog and the Passion," *America*, 112 (March 27, 1965): 425-427.

311. Detweiler, R. "Patterns of Rebirth in *Henderson the Rain King*," *MFS*, 12 (1966-67): 405-414.

312. Donoghue, D. "Commitment and the Dangling Man," *Studies*, 52 (1964): 174-187.

313. Eisinger, C. E. "Saul Bellow: Love and Identity," *Accent*, 18 (1958): 179-203.

314. Fisch, H. "The Hero as Jew; Reflections on *Herzog*," *Judaism*, 17 (1968): 42-54.

315. Fossum, R. H. "The Devil and Saul Bellow," *CLS*, 3 (1966): 197-206. [Collected in *Mansions of the Spirit*, ed. by G. A. Panichas, pp. 345-357. See item 770.]

316. Galloway, D. D. "The Absurd Man as Picaro: The Novels of Saul Bellow," *TSLL*, 6 (1964): 226-254. [Also in *The Absurd Hero in American Fiction*, by D. D. Galloway. See item 79.]

317. Markos, D. W. "Life Against Death in *Henderson the Rain King*," *MFS*, 17 (1971): 193-205.

318. Scott, N. A., Jr. *"Sola Gratia*—The Principle of Bellow's Fiction," in *Adversity and Grace*, pp. 27-57. See item 28.
See also 286, 290, 932, 968, 1022, 1023.

GEORGES BERNANOS

319. Champigny, R. "Spirits in Fiction: The Example of Bernanos," in *The Vision Obscured*, ed. by M. J. Friedman, pp. 129-139. See item 111.

320. Davies, H. *A Mirror of the Ministry in Modern Novels*, pp. 85-93. See item 131.

321. "Religion and Esthetic Values," *Commonweal*, 71 (1959): 155-167. See especially "Bernanos and the Modern Threat."
See also 118, 292, 293, 295, 919.

ALBERT CAMUS

322. Berger P. "Camus, Bonhoeffer, and the World Come of Age," *ChrC* (April 8, 1959 and April 15, 1959): 417-418, 450-452. [Collected in *Religion and Contemporary Western Culture*, ed. by E. Cell. New York & Nashville: Abingdon, 1967, pp. 194-199.]

323. Brée, G., ed. *Camus: A Collection of Critical Essays.* Englewood Cliffs, N.J.: Prentice-Hall, Inc., 1962.

324. Brockmann, C. B. "Metamorphoses of Hell: The Spiritual Quandary in *La Chute.*" *FR,* 35 (1962): 361-368.

325. Bryant, R. H. "Albert Camus' Quest for Ethical Values," *RIL,* 29 (1960): 443-452.

326. Burke, E. L. "Camus and the Pursuit of Happiness," *Thought,* 37 (1962): 391-409.

327. Cruickshank, J. "Albert Camus: Sainthood Without God," in *Mansions of the Spirit: Essays in Literature and Religion,* ed. by G. A. Panichas, pp. 313-324. See item 770.

328. Durfee, H. A. "Albert Camus and the Ethics of Rebellion," *JR,* 38 (1958): 29-45.

329. Glicksberg, C. I. "Camus's Quest for God," *SoWestR,* 44 (1959): 241-250. [Collected in *Literature and Religion: A Study in Conflict,* pp. 212-222. See item 747.]

330. Hamilton, W. "The Christian, the Saint, and the Rebel: Albert Camus," in *Forms of Extremity in the Modern Novel,* ed. by N. A. Scott, Jr., pp. 55-74. See item 30.

331. Hanna, T. L. "Albert Camus and the Christian Faith," *JR,* 36 (1956): 224-233. [Collected in *Camus: A Collection of Critical Essays,* ed. by G. Brée, pp. 48-58. See item 323.]

332. Hanna, T. L. *The Lyrical Existentialists.* New York: Atheneum [1962]. See especially Part III: Albert Camus: The Tender Indifference, pp. 187-274.

333. Hanna, T. L. "The Religious Significance of Camus' *The Fall,*" in *Religion and Contemporary Western Culture,* ed. by E. Cell. Nashville & New York: Abingdon, 1967, pp. 199-207.

334. Hanna, T. L. *The Thought and Art of Albert Camus.* Chicago: Henry Regnery Company, 1958.

335. Hardré, J. "Camus' Thoughts on Christian Metaphysics and Neo-Platonism," *SIP,* 64 (1967): 97-108. [All direct quotations from Camus are in French.]

336. Hartsock, M. "Camus' *The Fall:* Dialogue of One." *MFS,* 7 (1961-62): 357-364.

337. Hopper, S. R. "Camus: The Argument from the Absurd," in *Christian Faith and the Contemporary Arts,* ed. by F. Eversole, pp. 121-131. See item 800.

338. Ladd, G. "Rebellion and the Death of Hope: A Study of *The Plague,*" *RIL,* 39 (1970): 371-381.

339. Lakich, J. J. "Tragedy and Satanism in Camus's *La Chute,"* *Symposium,* 24 (1970) : 262-276.

340. Lauer, Q. "Albert Camus: The Revolt Against Absurdity," *Thought,* 35 (1960) : 37-56.

341. Loose, J. "The Christian as Camus's Absurd Man," *JR,* 42 (1962) : 203-214.

342. Mackey, J. P. "Christianity and Albert Camus," *Studies,* 55 (1966) : 392-402.

343. Madden, D. "Ambiguity in Albert Camus' *The Fall,"* *MFS,* 12 (1966-67) : 461-472.

344. May, W. F. "Albert Camus, Political Moralist," *C&C,* 18 (1958) : 165-168.

345. Merton, T. "Three Saviors in Camus," *Thought,* 43 (1968) : 5-23.

346. Moeller, C. "Albert Camus: the Question of Hope," *CrCur,* 8 (1958) : 172-184.

347. Mueller, W. R. "The Theme of the Fall: Albert Camus's *The Fall,"* in *The Prophetic Voice in Modern Fiction,* by W. R. Mueller, pp. 56-82. See item 22.

348. Murchland, B. G. "Albert Camus: The Dark Night Before the Coming of Grace?" in *Camus: A Collection of Critical Essays,* ed. by G. Brée, pp. 59-64. See item 323. [Originally titled "Albert Camus: Rebel," in *CathW,* 188 (1959) : 308-314.]

349. Onimus, J. *Albert Camus and Christianity.* Tr. by E. Parker. University, Alabama: University of Alabama Press, 1970.

350. Petrey, S. "The Function of Christian Imagery in *La Chute,"* *TSLL,* 11 (1970) : 1445-1454.

351. Peyre, H. "Camus the Pagan," in *Camus: A Collection of Critical Essays,* ed. by G. Brée, pp. 65-70. See item 323. [Originally printed in *YFS,* 25 (1960) : 20-25.]

352. St. Amant, P. "God, Man and Redemption in the Writings of Albert Camus," *R&E,* 61 (1964) : 156-166.

353. Scott, N. A., Jr. *Albert Camus.* Studies in Modern European Literature and Thought Series. London: Bowes & Bowes Ltd., 1962; New York: Hillary House, 1962.

354. Scott, N. A., Jr. "The Modest Optimism of Albert Camus," *ChrS,* 42 (1959) : 251-274.

355. Singleton, M. "Teilhard on Camus," *IPQ,* 9 (1969) : 236-247.

356. Starratt, R. J. "An Analysis of Albert Camus' *The Fall*," *Cithara*, 1 (1961): 27-38.

357. Stourzh, G. "The Unforgiveable Sin: An Interpretation of *The Fall*," *ChiR* 15, i (1961): 45-57.

358. Terrien, S. "Christianity's Debt to a Modern Pagan, Albert Camus (1913-1960)," *USQR*, 15 (1960): 185-194.

359. Yalom, M. K. *"La Chute* and *A Hero Of Our Time,"* *FR*, 36 (1962): 138-145.

360. Yu, A. C. *"La Pureté Fugitive:* The Experience of the Fall in Camus' *La Chute,"* *USQR*, 25 (1970): 287-310.
    See also 19, 64, 81, 176, 271, 295, 919, 959, 966, 997.

TRUMAN CAPOTE

361. Levine, P. "Truman Capote: The Revelation of the Broken Image," *VQR*, 34 (1958): 600-617.
    See also 278.

JOYCE CARY

362. Bloom, R. *The Indeterminate World: A Study of the Novels of Joyce Cary.* Philadelphia: University of Pennsylvania Press, 1962.

363. Brawer, J. "The Triumph of Defeat: A Study of Joyce Cary's *First Trilogy,"* *TSLL*, 10 (1969): 629-634.

364. Cohen, N., interviewer. "A Conversation with Joyce Cary," *TamR*, No. 3 (Spring 1957): 5-15.

365. Larsen, G. L. *The Dark Descent*[:] *Social Change and Moral Responsibility in the Novels of Joyce Cary.* London: Michael Joseph, 1965. See especially pp. 180-193.

366. Salz, P. J. "The Philosophical Principles in Joyce Cary's Work," *WHR*, 20 (1966): 159-165.

367. Stewart, D. "Joyce Cary—Protestantism," in *The Ark of God,* pp. 129-158. See item 296.

368. Wolkenfeld, J. *Joyce Cary*[:] *The Developing Style.* New York: New York University Press, 1968. See especially pp. 157-191.
    See also 1015.

ROBERT COOVER

369. Hertzel, L. J. "What's Wrong with the Christians?", *Crit*, 11, iii (1969): 11-22.

PETER DeVRIES

370. Davies, H. *A Mirror of the Ministry in Modern Novels,* pp. 164-172. See item 131.

371. Hamblen, A. A. "Peter DeVries: Calvinist Gone Underground," *Trace,* #48 (Spring 1963): 20-24.

372. Jellema, R. *Peter DeVries.* Contemporary Writers in Christian Perspective Series. Grand Rapids, Michigan: Wm. B. Eerdmans, 1967.
See also 291.

WILLIAM FAULKNER

373. Barth, J. R. "A Rereading of Faulkner's *Fable,*" *America,* 92 (1954): 44-46.

374. Barth, J. R. "Faulkner and the Calvinist Tradition," *Thought,* 39 (1964): 100-120.

375. Björk, L. "Ancient Myths and the Moral Framework of Faulkner's *Absalom, Absalom!*" *AL,* 35 (1963): 196-204.

376. Blotner, J. *"As I Lay Dying:* Christian Lore and Irony," *TCL,* 3 (1957): 14-19.

377. Brooks, C. *William Faulkner: The Yoknapatawpha County.* New Haven: Yale University Press, 1963.

378. Burrows, R. N. "Institutional Christianity as Reflected in the Works of William Faulkner," *MissQ,* 14 (1961): 138-147.

379. Cottrell, B. "Christian Symbols in *Light in August,*" *MFS,* 2 (1956-57): 207-213.

380. Doyle, C. "The Moral World of Faulkner," *Renascence,* 19 (1966): 3-12.

381. Gold, J. "Delusion and Redemption in Faulkner's *A Fable,*" *MFS,* 7 (1961): 145-156.

382. Greene, T. M. "The Philosophy of Life Implicit in Faulkner's *The Mansion,*" *TSLL,* 2 (1961): 401-418.

383. Hartt, J. N. "Some Reflections on Faulkner's *Fable,*" *RIL,* 24 (1955): 601-607.

384. Hunt, J. W. *William Faulkner: Art in Theological Tension.* Syracuse University Press, 1965.

385. Kunkel, F. L. "Christ Symbolism in Faulkner: Prevalence of the Human," *Renascence,* 16 (1965): 148-156.

386. Lewis, R. W. B. "The Hero in the New World," *KR*, 13 (1951): 641-660.

387. Lind, I. D. "Calvinistic Burden of *Light in August*," *NEQ*, 30 (1957): 307-329.

388. McGehee, L. T. "The Southern Ethic of William Faulkner," *Encounter*, 26 (1965): 461-469.

389. Mellard, J. M. "The Biblical Rhythm of *Go Down Moses*," *MissQ*, 20 (1967): 135-147.

390. Miller, J. E. "William Faulkner: Descent into the Vortex," in *Quests Surd and Absurd*, pp. 41-65. See item 82.

391. Mills, R. J., Jr. "Faulkner's Essential Vision: Notes on *A Fable*," *ChrS*, 44 (1961): 187-198.

392. Mueller, W. R. "The Theme of Suffering: William Faulkner's *The Sound and the Fury*," in *The Prophetic Voice in Modern Fiction*, pp. 110-135. See item 22.

393. O'Dea, R. J. "Faulkner's Vestigial Christianity," *Renascence*, 21 (1968): 44-54.

394. Penick, E. A., Jr. "The Testimony of William Faulkner," *ChrS*, 38 (1955): 121-133.

395. Sandeen, E. "William Faulkner: His Legend and His Fable," *RevP*, 18 (1956): 47-68.

396. Sandeen, E. "William Faulkner: Tragedian of Yoknapatawpha," in *Fifty Years of the American Novel*, ed. by H. C. Gardiner, pp. 165-181. See item 170.

397. Smart, G. K. *Religious Elements in Faulkner's Early Novels*. Miami, Florida: University of Miami Press, 1965. [A concordance.]

398. Strandberg, V. "Faulkner's Poor Parson and the Technique of Inversion," *SR*, 73 (1965): 181-190.

399. Yu, A. C. "Faulkner's Hightower: The Allergy to History," *ATR*, 52 (1970): 42-52.
    See also 19, 72, 189, 284, 287, 298, 897, 911, 918, 969, 989, 1010.

WILLIAM GOLDING

400. Biles, J. I. and C. R. Kropf. "The Cleft Rock of Conversion: *Robinson Crusoe* and *Pincher Martin*," *SLitI*, 2 (1969): 17-43.

401. Braybrooke, N. "Return of Pincher Martin," *Commonweal*, 89 (1968): 115-118.

402. Braybrooke, N. "Two William Golding Novels: Two Aspects of His Work," *QQ*, 76 (1969): 92-100.

403. Broes, A. T. "The Two Worlds of William Golding," in *Lectures on Modern Novelists* (CaSE #7). Pittsburgh: Department of English, Carnegie Institute of Technology, 1963, pp. 1-14.

404. Bufkin, E. C. *"Pincher Martin:* William Golding's Morality Play," *SLitI*, 2 (1969): 5-16.

405. Coskren, T. M. "Is Golding Calvinistic?" *America*, 109 (1963): 18-20.

406. Cox, C. B. "Lord of the Flies," *CritQ*, 2 (1960): 112-117.

407. Egan, J. M. "Golding's View of Man," *America*, 108 (1963): 140-141.

408. Elmen, P. "Prince of the Devils," *C&C*, 23 (1963): 7-10.

409. Elmen, P. *William Golding.* Contemporary Writers in Christian Perspective Series. Grand Rapids, Michigan: William B. Eerdmans, 1967.

410. Gallagher, M. P. "The Human Image in William Golding," *Studies*, 54 (1965): 197-216.

411. Gaskin, J. C. A. "Beelzebub," *HJ*, 66 (1967-68): 58-61.

412. Green, P. "The World of William Golding," *REL*, 1 (1960): 62-72.

413. Gregor, I. and M. Kinkead-Weekes, "The Strange Case of Mr. Golding and His Critics," *TC*, 167 (1960): 115-125.

414. Hynes, S. "Novels of a Religious Man," *Commonweal*, 71 (1960): 673-675.

415. La Chance, P. R. "Pincher Martin: The Essential Dilemma of Modern Man," *Cithara*, 8 (1969): 55-60.

416. McKeating, H. "Significance of William Golding," *ExpT*, 79 (1968): 329-333.

417. Mueller, W. R. "An Old Story Well Told: Commentary on William Goldings' *Lord of the Flies*," *ChrC*, 80 (1963): 1203-1206. Reply by V. Eller in *ChrC*, 80 (1963): 1440.

418. Sternlicht, S. "The Sin of Pride in Golding's *The Spire*," *MinnR*, 5 (1965): 59-60.

419. Stinson, J. J. "Trying to Exorcise the Beast: The Grotesque in the Fiction of William Golding," *Cithara*, 11 (1971): 3-30.

420. Sullivan, W. "The Long Chronicle of Guilt: William Golding's *The Spire," HC,* 1 (1964) : 1-12.

421. Thomson, G. H. "William Golding: Between God-Darkness and God-Light," *Cresset,* 32 (1969) : 8-12.

422. Whitehead, L. M. "The Moment Out of Time: Golding's *Pincher Martin," ConL,* 12 (1971) : 18-41.
    See also 280, 289, 994.

CAROLINE GORDON

423. Brown, A. "The Novel as Christian Comedy," in *Reality and Myth,* ed. by W. E. Walker and R. L. Walker. Nashville: Vanderbilt University Press, 1964, pp. 161-178.

424. Cheney, B. "Caroline Gordon's Ontological Quest," *Renascence,* 16 (1963) : 3-12.

425. Cheney, B. "Caroline Gordon's *The Malefactors," SR,* 79 (1971) : 360-372.

426. Cowan, L. "Nature and Grace in Caroline Gordon," *Crit,* 1, i (1956) : 11-27.

427. Rocks, J. E. "The Christian Myth as Salvation: Caroline Gordon's *The Strange Children," TuSE,* 16 (1968) : 149-160.

GRAHAM GREENE

428. Birmingham, W. "Graham Greene Criticism: A Bibliographical Study," *Thought,* 27 (1952) : 72-100.

429. Cargas, H. J. *Graham Greene.* The Christian Critic Series. St. Louis: B. Herder Book Company, 1969.

430. Chapman, R. "The Vision of Graham Greene," in *Forms of Extremity in the Modern Novel,* ed. by N. A. Scott, Jr., pp. 75-94. See item 30.

431. Cosman, M. "The Disquieted Graham Greene," *ColQ,* 6 (1958) : 319-325.

432. Costello, D. P. "Graham Greene and the Catholic Press," *Renascence,* 12 (1959) : 3-28.

433. Davies, H. *A Mirror of the Ministry in Modern Novels,* pp. 100-110. See item 131.

434. Desmond, J. F. "Graham Greene and the Eternal Dimension," *ABR,* 20 (1969) : 418-427.

435. DeVitis, A. A. 'The Catholic as Novelist: Graham Greene and François Mauriac," in *Graham Greene: Some Critical Considerations,* ed. by R. O. Evans, pp. 112-126. See item 439.

436. DeVitis, A. A. "The Church and Major Scobie," *Renascence,* 10 (1958): 115-120.

437. DeVitis, A. A. "Religious Aspects in the Novels of Graham Greene," in *The Shapeless God,* ed. by H. J. Mooney and T. F. Staley, pp. 41-65. See item 20.

438. Ellis, W. D., Jr. "The Grand Theme of Graham Greene," *SoWestR,* 41 (1956): 239-250.

439. Evans, R. O., ed. *Graham Greene: Some Critical Considerations.* Lexington, Kentucky: University of Kentucky Press, 1963.

440. Evans, R. O. "The Satanist Fallacy of *Brighton Rock,"* in *Graham Greene: Some Critical Considerations,* ed. by R. O. Evans, pp. 151-168. See item 439.

441. Glicksberg, C. I. "Graham Greene: Catholicism in Fiction," *Criticism,* 1 (1959): 339-353.

442. Grob, A. *"The Power and the Glory:* Graham Greene's Argument From Design," *Criticism,* 11 (1969): 1-30.

443. Haber, H. R. "The End of the Catholic Cycle: The Writer Versus the Saint," in *Graham Greene: Some Critical Considerations,* ed. by R. O. Evans, pp. 127-150. See item 439.

444. Hesla, D. H. "Theological Ambiguity in the 'Catholic Novels'," in *Graham Greene: Some Critical Considerations,* ed. by R. O. Evans, pp. 96-111. See item 439.

445. Hortmann, W. "Graham Greene: The Burnt-Out Catholic," *TCL,* 10 (1964): 64-76.

446. Houle, Sister S. "The Subjective Theological Vision of Graham Greene," *Renascence,* 23 (1970-71): 3-13.

447. Jones, G. C. "Graham Greene and the Legend of Péguy." *CL,* 21 (1969): 138-145.

448. Kermode, F. "Mr. Greene's Eggs and Crosses," *Encounter,* 16 (1961): 69-75.

449. Kort, W. "The Obsession of Graham Greene," *Thought,* 45 (1970): 20-44.

450. Kunkel, F. L. "The Theme of Sin and Grace in Graham Greene," in *Graham Greene: Some Critical Considerations,* ed. by R. O. Evans, pp. 49-60. See item 439.

451. Marian, Sister. "Graham Greene's People: Being and Becoming," *Renascence,* 18 (1965): 16-22.

452. Marković, V. E. "Graham Greene in Search of God," *TSLL*, 5 (1963) : 271-282.

453. Mueller, W. R. "The Theme of Love: Graham Greene's *The Heart of the Matter*," in *The Prophetic Voice in Modern Fiction*, pp. 136-157. See item 22.

454. Noxon, J. "Kierkegaard's Stages and 'A Burnt-Out Case'," *REL*, 3 (1962) : 90-101.

455. Rolo, C. J. "Graham Greene: The Man and the Message," *Atlan*, 207 (May 1961) : 60-65.

456. Scott, N. A., Jr. "Graham Greene: Christian Tragedian," in *Graham Greene: Some Critical Considerations*, ed. by R. O. Evans, pp. 25-48. See item 439.

457. Sewell, E. "The Imagination of Graham Greene," *Thought*, 29 (1954) : 51-60.

458. Smith, A. J. M. "Graham Greene's Theological Thrillers," *QQ*, 68 (1961) : 15-33.

459. Sonnenfeld, A. "Children's Faces: Graham Greene," in *The Vision Obscured*, ed. by M. J. Friedman, pp. 109-127. See item 111.

460. Stewart, D. "Graham Greene—Catholicism," in *The Ark of God*, pp. 71-98. See item 296.

461. Turnell, M. *Graham Greene*. Contemporary Writers in Christian Perspective Series. Grand Rapids, Michigan: Wm. B. Eerdmans, 1967.

462. Wassmer, T. A. "Faith and Reason in Graham Greene," *Studies*, 48 (1959) : 163-167.

463. Wassmer, T. A. "Graham Greene: A Look at His Sinners," *Critic*, 18 (1960) : 16-17, 72-74.

464. Wassmer, T. A. "The Problem and Mystery of Sin in the Works of Graham Greene," *ChrS*, 43 (1960) : 309-315.

465. Wassmer, T. A. "The Sinners of Graham Greene," *DR*, 39 (1959) : 326-332.

466. White, W. D. "*The Power and the Glory:* An Apology to the Church," *UPR*, 21 (1969) : 14-22.

467. Wichert, R. A. "The Quality of Graham Greene's Mercy," *CE*, 25 (1963) : 99-103.
     See also 19, 118, 281, 288, 292, 293, 295, 297, 299, 300, 903, 928, 940, 956, 959.

JOHN HAWKES

468. Matthews, C. "The Destructive Vision of John Hawkes," *Crit*, 6, ii (1963): 38-52.
      See also 1001, 1016.

JOSEPH HELLER

469. Hunt, J. W. "Comic Escape and Anti-Vision: The Novels of Joseph Heller and Thomas Pynchon," in *Adversity and Grace*, ed. by N. A. Scott, Jr., pp. 87-111. See item 28.

470. Milne, V. J. "Heller's Bologniad: A Theological Perspective on *Catch-22*," *Crit*, 12, ii (1970): 50-69.

471. Solomon, E. "From Christ in Flanders to *Catch-22*: An Approach to War Fiction," *TSLL*, 11 (1969): 851-866.
      See also 144, 177, 979, 1001.

ERNEST HEMINGWAY

472. Backman, M. "Hemingway: The Matador and the Crucified," *MFS*, 1 (1955): 2-11. [Collected in *Hemingway and His Critics: An International Anthology*, ed. by C. Baker. New York: Hill & Wang, 1961, pp. 248-258.]

473. Baker, C. *Hemingway[:] The Writer as Artist*. Princeton: Princeton University Press, 1963. See especially pp. 289-328.

474. Bradford, M. E. "On the Importance of Discovering God: Faulkner and Hemingway's *The Old Man and the Sea*," *MissQ*, 20 (1967): 158-162.

475. Burhans, C. S., Jr. *"The Old Man and the Sea:* Hemingway's Tragic Vision of Man," *AL*, 31 (1960): 446-455. [Collected in *Hemingway and His Critics: An International Anthology*, ed. by C. Baker. New York: Hill & Wang, 1961, pp. 259-268.]

476. Hertzel, L. J. "The Look of Religion: Hemingway and Catholicism," *Renascence*, 17 (1964): 77-81.

477. Isabelle, J. *Hemingway's Religious Experience*. New York: Vantage Press, 1964.

478. Killinger, J. "Hemingway and our 'Essential Worldliness'," in *Forms of Extremity in the Modern Novel*, ed. by N. A. Scott, Jr., pp. 35-45. See item 30.

479. Light, J. F. "The Religion of Death in *A Farewell to Arms*," *MFS*, 7 (1961): 169-173. [Collected in *Ernest Hemingway: Critiques of Four Major Novels*, ed. by C. Baker. New York: Scribner's Sons, 1962, pp. 37-40.]

480. Moloney, M. F. "Ernest Hemingway: The Missing Third Dimension," in *Fifty Years of the American Novel*, ed. by H. Gardiner, pp. 183-196. See item 170.

481. Scott, N. A., Jr. *Ernest Hemingway*. Contemporary Writers in Christian Perspective Series. Grand Rapids, Michigan: Wm. B. Eerdmans, 1966.

482. Smith, J. "Christ Times Four: Hemingway's Unknown Spanish Civil War Stories," *ArQ*, 25 (1969): 5-17.

483. Waggoner, H. H. "Ernest Hemingway," *ChrS*, 38 (1955): 114-120.

484. Waldmeir, J. J. "Confiteor Hominem: Ernest Hemingway's Religion of Man," in *Hemingway: A Collection of Critical Essays*, ed. by R. P. Weeks, pp. 161-168. See item 485.

485. Weeks, R. P., ed. *Hemingway: A Collection of Critical Essays*. Englewood Cliffs, N.J.: Prentice-Hall, Inc., 1962.

486. Wells, A. R. "Ritual of Transfiguration; *The Old Man and the Sea*," *UR*, 30 (1963): 95-101.
    See also 161, 281, 284, 922, 939.

NIKOS KAZANTZAKIS

487. Banks, A. C., Jr. and F. C. Campbell. "The Vision of the Negro in the Kazantzakian Universe," *Phylon*, 25 (1964): 254-262.

488. Calihan, C. S. "Kazantzakis: Prophet of Non-hope," *ThT*, 28 (1971): 37-49.

489. Stavrou, C. N. "Some Notes on Nikos Kazantzakis," *ColQ*, 12 (1964): 317-334.
    See also 72, 287, 902.

KEN KESEY

See 68, 1001.

ARTHUR KOESTLER

490. Fossum, R. H. "The Defective Christ of Arthur Koestler," *ChrS*, 41 (1958): 555-561.
    See also 280.

GERTRUD VON LEFORT

491. Hilton, I. "Gertrud Von LeFort—A Christian Writer," *GL&L*, 15 n.s. (1962): 300-307.
    See also 295.

CARSON McCULLERS

492. Durham, F. "God and No God in *The Heart is a Lonely Hunter*," *SAQ*, 56 (1957): 494-499.

493. Mathis, R. "Reflections in a Golden Eye: Myth-making in American Christianity," *RIL*, 39 (1970): 545-558.
See also 278, 920.

NORMAN MAILER

494. Hesla, D. "The Two Roles of Norman Mailer," in *Adversity and Grace*, ed. by N. A. Scott, Jr., pp. 211-237. See item 28.

495. Schrader, G. A. "Norman Mailer and the Despair of Defiance," *YR*, 51 (1962): 267-281.

496. Schroth, R. A. "Mailer and His Gods," *Commonweal*, 90 (1969): 226-229.

497. Schulz, M. F. "Mailer's Divine Comedy," *ConL*, 9 (1968): 36-57.
See also 286, 1018.

BERNARD MALAMUD

498. Baumbach, J. "The Economy of Love: the Novels of Bernard Malamud," *KR*, 25 (1963): 438-457.

499. Drake, R. "Signs of the Times or Signs for All Times?" *ChrC*, 85 (1968): 1204-1206.

500. Field, L. A. and J. W. Field, eds. *Bernard Malamud and the Critics*. New York & London: New York University/University of London Press Ltd., 1970.

501. Gunn, G. B. "Bernard Malamud and the High Cost of Living," in *Adversity and Grace*, ed. by N. A. Scott, Jr., pp. 59-85. See item 28.

502. Hays, P. L. "The Complex Pattern of Redemption in *The Assistant*," *CentR*, 13 (1969): 200-214.

503. Mandel, R. B. "Bernard Malamud's *The Assistant* and *A New Life:* Ironic Affirmation," *Crit*, 7, ii (1964-65): 110-122.

504. Meeter, G. *Philip Roth/Bernard Malamud*. Contemporary Writers in Christian Perspective Series. Grand Rapids, Michigan: Wm. B. Eerdmans, 1968.

505. Pinsker, S. "The Achievement of Bernard Malamud," *MQ*, 10 (1969): 379-389.

506. Standley, F. L. "Bernard Malamud: The Novels of Redemption," *SHR*, 5 (1971): 309-318.

507. Warburton, R. W. "Fantasy and the Fiction of Bernard Malamud," in *Imagination and the Spirit*, ed. by C. Huttar, pp. 387-416. See item 757.
See also 83, 282, 290, 291.

FRANÇOIS MAURIAC

508. Brée, G. "The Novels of François Mauriac," in *The Vision Obscured*, ed. by M. J. Friedman, pp. 141-149. See item 111.

509. Caspary, Sister A. M. *François Mauriac*. Christian Critic Series. St. Louis: Herder, 1968.

510. Davies, H. *A Mirror of the Ministry in Modern Novels*, pp. 93-100. See item 131.

511. DeVitis, A. A. "The Catholic as Novelist: Graham Greene and François Mauriac," in *Graham Greene: Some Critical Considerations*, ed. by R. O. Evans, pp. 112-126. See item 439.

512. Fowlie, W. "The Christian Critic and Mauriac," in *The Climate of Violence*. New York: Macmillan Company, 1967, pp. 235-248.

513. Jarrett-Kerr, M. *Mauriac*. Studies in Modern European Literature and Thought. London: Bowes & Bowes, 1954.

514. Mein, M. "François Mauriac and Jansenism," *MLR*, 58 (1963): 516-523.

515. Moloney, M. F. "François Mauriac: The Way of Pascal," *Thought*, 32 (1957): 398-408.

516. "Religion and Esthetic Values," *Commonweal*, 71 (1959): 155-167. See especially "Mauriac on His Novels" and "Mauriac and Gide: Great Adversaries."

517. Rubin, L. D., Jr. "François Mauriac and the Freedom of the Religious Novelist," *SoR*, 2 n.s. (1966): 17-39.

518. Rubin, L. D., Jr. "François Mauriac; or The Novelist as Theologian," in *The Teller in the Tale*, by L. D. Rubin, Jr. Seattle & London: University of Washington Press, 1967, pp. 178-210.

519. Stratford, P. "François Mauriac and His Critics," *TamR*, No. 3 (Spring 1957): 64-77.

520. Stratford, P. "One Meeting with Mauriac," *KR*, 21 (1959): 611-622.

521. Vial, F. "François Mauriac Criticism: A Bibliographical Study," *Thought*, 27 (1952): 235-260.
See also 72, 118, 260, 292, 293, 295, 297, 299, 300, 941, 1000.

HENRY MILLER

522. Polley, G. W. "The Art of Religious Writing: Henry Miller as Religious Writer," *SDR*, 7 (1969): 61-73.

VLADIMIR NABOKOV

523. Green, M. B. "The Morality of *Lolita*," in *Yeats's Blessings on von Hügel*, pp. 128-155. See item 113.
     See also 1025.

EDWIN O'CONNOR

524. Rank, H. "O'Connor's Image of the Priest," *NEQ*, 41 (1968): 3-29.

FLANNERY O'CONNOR

525. Asals, F. "Mythic Dimensions of Flannery O'Connor's 'Greenleaf'," *SSF*, 5 (1968): 317-330.

526. Bassan, M. "Flannery O'Connor's Way: Shock with Moral Intent," *Renascence*, 15 (1963): 195-199.

527. Baumbach, J. "The Acid of God's Grace: the Fiction of Flannery O'Connor," *GeorR*, 17 (1963): 334-346. [Collected in *The Landscape of Nightmare: Studies in the Contemporary American Novel*, pp. 87-100. See item 282.]

528. Bergup, Sister B. "Themes of Redemptive Grace in the Works of Flannery O'Connor," *ABR*, 21 (1970): 169-191.

529. Bertrande, Sister. "Four Stories of Flannery O'Connor," *Thought*, 37 (1962): 410-426.

530. Browning, P. M., Jr. "Flannery O'Connor and the Grotesque Recovery of the Holy," in *Adversity and Grace*, ed. by N. A. Scott, Jr., pp. 133-161. See item 28.

531. Browning, P. M., Jr. "'Parker's Back': Flannery O'Connor's Iconography of Salvation by Profanity," *SSF*, 6 (1969): 525-535.

532. Burke, J. J., Jr. "The Convergence of Flannery O'Connor and Chardin," *Renascence*, 19 (1966): 41-47.

533. Burns, S. L. "Flannery O'Connor's *The Violent Bear It Away*: Apotheosis in Failure," *SR*, 76 (1968): 319-336.

534. Burns, S. L. "'Torn by the Lord's Eye': Flannery O'Connor's Use of Sun Imagery," *TCL*, 13 (1967): 154-166.

535. Byrd, T. F. "Ironic Dimension in Flannery O'Connor's 'The Artificial Nigger'," *MissQ*, 21 (1968): 243-251.

536. Carlson, T. M. "Flannery O'Connor: the Manichaean Dilemma," *SR*, 77 (1969): 254-276.

537. Cheney, B. "Miss O'Connor Creates Unusual Humor Out of Ordinary Sin," *SR*, 71 (1963): 644-652.

538. Coffey, W. "Flannery O'Connor," *Commentary,* 40 (1965): 94-99.

539. Davis, B. "Flannery O'Connor: Christian Belief in Recent Fiction," *Listening,* 1 (1965): 5-21.

540. Detweiler, R. "The Curse of Christ in Flannery O'Connor's Fiction," *CLS,* 3 (1966): 235-245. [Collected in *Mansions of the Spirit,* ed. by G. A. Panichas, pp. 372-386. See item 770.]

541. Dowell, B. "The Moment of Grace in the Fiction of Flannery O'Connor," *CE,* 27 (1965): 235-239.

542. Drake, R. "The Bleeding Stinking Mad Shadow of Jesus' in the Fiction of Flannery O'Connor," *CLS,* 3 (1966): 183-196.

543. Drake, R. *Flannery O'Connor.* Contemporary Writers in Christian Perspective Series. Grand Rapids, Michigan: William B. Eerdmans, 1966.

544. Drake, R. "The Harrowing Evangel of Flannery O'Connor," *ChrC,* 81 (1964): 1200-1202. [Reprinted in *Esprit,* 8 (1964): 19-22.]

545. Drake, R. "Miss O'Connor and the Scandal of Redemption," *ModA,* 4 (1960): 428-430.

546. Eggenschwiler, D. "Flannery O'Connor's True and False Prophets," *Renascence,* 21 (1969): 151-161.

547. Ferris, S. J. "The Outside and the Inside: Flannery O'Connor's *The Violent Bear It Away,*" *Crit,* 3, ii (1960): 11-19.

548. Fitzgerald, R. "The Countryside and the True Country," *SR,* 70 (1962): 380-394.

549. Fitzgerald, R. "Introduction" to *Everything That Rises Must Converge* by Flannery O'Connor. A Signet Book published by the New American Library, 1967: vii-xxiv. First printed, Farrar, Straus and Giroux, Inc., 1956.

550. Friedman, M. J. and L. A. Lawson, eds., *The Added Dimension[:] The Art and Mind of Flannery O'Connor.* New York: Fordham University Press, 1966.

551. Friedman, M. J. "Flannery O'Connor's Sacred Objects," in *The Vision Obscured,* pp. 67-77. See item 111.

552. Gable, Sister M. "The Ecumenic Core in the Fiction of Flannery O'Connor," *ABR,* 15 (1964): 127-143.

553. Gordon, C. "Flannery O'Connor's *Wise Blood,*" *Crit,* 2, ii (1958): 3-10.

554. Griffith, A. J. "Flannery O'Connor's Salvation Road," *SSF*, 3 (1966) : 329-333.

555. Hawkes, J. "Flannery O'Connor's Devil," *SR*, 70 (1962) : 395-407.

556. Lawson, L. A. "Flannery O'Connor and the Grotesque: *Wise Blood*," *Renascence*, 17 (1965) : 137-147. [Collected in *Flannery O'Connor*, ed. by R. Reiter, pp.51-67. See item 571.]

557. Lensing, G. "De Chardin's Ideas in Flannery O'Connor," *Renascence*, 18 (1966) : 171-175.

558. Littlefield, D. F., Jr. "Flannery O'Connor's *Wise Blood:* Unparalleled Prosperity and Spiritual Chaos," *MissQ*, 23 (1970) : 121-133.

559. Lorch, T. M. "Flannery O'Connor: Christian Allegorist," *Crit*, 10, ii (1968) : 69-80.

560. Lorentzen, M. E. "A Good Writer Is Hard to Find," in *Imagination and the Spirit*, ed. by C. Huttar, pp. 417-435. See item 757.

561. McCarthy, J. F. "Human Intelligence versus Divine Truth: The Intellectual in Flannery O'Connor's Works," EJ, 55 (1966) : 1143-1148.

562. Marks, W. S., III. "Advertisements for Grace: Flannery O'Connor's 'A Good Man is Hard to Find'," *SSF*, 4 (1966) : 19-27.

563. Montgomery, M. "Flannery O'Connor and the Natural Man," *MissQ*, 21 (1968) : 235-242.

564. Montgomery, M. "Flannery O'Connor's Territorial Center," *Crit*, 11, iii (1969) : 5-10.

565. Montgomery, M. "Miss O'Connor and the Christ-Haunted," *SoR*, 4 n.s. (1968) : 665-672.

566. Montgomery, M. "O'Connor and Teilhard de Chardin: The Problem of Evil," *Renascence*, 22 (1969) : 34-42.

567. Mooney, H. J., Jr. "Moments of Eternity: A Study in the Short Stories of Flannery O'Connor," in *The Shapeless God*, ed. by H. J. Mooney and T. F. Staley, pp. 117-137. See item 20.

568. Nolde, M. S. *"The Violent Bear It Away:* A Study in Imagery," *XUS*, 1 (1961-62) : 180-194.

569. O'Brien, J. T. "The Un-christianity of Flannery O'Connor," *Listening* (1971) : 71-82.

570. O'Connor, F. "The Fiction Writer and His Country," in *The Living Novel: a symposium*, ed. by G. Hicks. New York: The Macmillan Company, 1957, pp. 157-164.

571. Reiter, R. E., ed. *Flannery O'Connor.* Christian Critic Series. St. Louis: B. Herder, 1968.

572. Rupp, R. H. "Flannery O'Connor," *Commonweal,* 79 (1963): 304-307.

573. Shinn, T. J. "Flannery O'Connor and the Violence of Grace," *ConL,* 9 (1968): 58-73.

574. Smith, F. J. "O'Connor's Religious Viewpoint in *The Violent Bear It Away,*" *Renascence,* 22 (1970): 108-112.

575. Smith, J. O. "Ritual and Violence in Flannery O'Connor," *Thought,* 41 (1966): 545-560.

576. Spivey, T. R. "Flannery O'Connor's View of God and Man," *SSF,* i (1964): 200-206. [Collected in *Flannery O'Connor,* ed. by R. Reiter, pp. 51-67. See item 571.]

577. Stelzmann, R. A. "Shock and Orthodoxy: An Interpretation of Flannery O'Connor's Novels and Short Stories," *XUS,* 2 (1963): 4-21.

578. Stephens, M. "Flannery O'Connor and the Sanctified-Sinner Tradition," *ArQ,* 24 (1968): 223-239.

579. Sullivan, W. "Flannery O'Connor, Sin and Grace: *Everything That Rises Must Converge,*" *HC,* 2 (1965): 1-8, 10.

580. Trowbridge, C. W. "The Symbolic Vision of Flannery O'Connor: Patterns of Imagery in *The Violent Bear It Away,*" *SR,* 76 (1968): 298-318.

581. True, M. D. "Flannery O'Connor: Backwoods Prophet in the Secular City," *PLL,* 5 (1969): 209-224.

582. Vande Kieft, R. M. "Judgment in the Fiction of Flannery O'Connor," *SR,* 76 (1968): 337-356.
   See also 68, 118, 278, 288, 294, 908, 909, 910, 926, 930, 931, 944, 945, 946, 955, 998, 1012.

GEORGE ORWELL

583. Scott, N. A., Jr. "The Example of George Orwell," *C&C,* 19 (1959): 107-110.
   See also 163.

BORIS PASTERNAK

584. Baird, Sister M. J. "Pasternak's Zhivago—Hamlet—Christ," *Renascence,* 14 (1962): 179-184.

585. Chakravarty, A. "Pasternak: Poet of Humanity," *ChrC,* 77 (1960): 803-804.

586. Green, M. B. *"Dr. Zhivago* and the Critics," in *Yeats's Blessings on von Hügel,* pp. 189-229. See item 113.

587. Grigorieff, D. F. "Pasternak and Dostoevskij," *Slavic and East European Journal,* 17 (1959): 335-342.

588. Iswolsky, H. "The Voice of Boris Pasternak," *Commonweal,* 69 (1958): 168-170.

589. Livingstone, A. "The Childhood of Luvers: An Early Story of Pasternak's," *SoR,* 1 (1963): 74-84.

590. Magidoff, R. "The Life, Times and Art of Boris Pasternak," *Thought,* 42 (1967): 327-357.

591. Moreau, J-L. "The Passion According to Zhivago," *BA,* 44 (1970): 237-242.

592. Panichas, G. A. "Boris Pasternak's Protest and Affirmation," *GOTR,* 4 (1958-59): 161-172.

WALKER PERCY

593. Atkins, A. "Walker Percy and Post-Christian Search," *CentR,* 12 (1968): 73-95.

594. Henisey, S. "Intersubjectivity in Symbolization," *Renascence,* 20 (1968): 208-214.

595. Kazin, A. "The Pilgrimage of Walker Percy," *Harper,* 242 (June 1972): 81-86.

596. Lawson, L. A. "Walker Percy's Indirect Communications," *TSLL,* 11 (1969): 867-900.

597. Lawson, L. A. "Walker Percy's Southern Stoic," *SLJ,* 3 (1970): 5-31.

598. Lehan, R. "The Way Back: Redemption in the Novels of Walker Percy," *SoR,* 4 n.s. (1968): 306-319.

599. Maxwell, R. "Walker Percy's Fancy," *MinnR,* 7 (1967): 231-237. See also 283, 907, 927, 976, 981, 995, 1017.

KATHERINE ANNE PORTER

600. Gottfried, L. "Death's Other Kingdom: Dantesque and Theological Symbolism in *Flowering Judas,*" *PMLA,* 84 (1969): 112-124.

601. Redden, D. S. " 'Flowering Judas': Two Voices," *SSF,* 6 (1969): 194-204.

J. F. POWERS

602. Bates, B. W. "Flares of Special Grace: The Orthodoxy of J. F. Powers," *MQ,* 11 (1969): 91-106.

603. Boyle, R. "To Look Outside: The Fiction of J. F. Powers," in *The Shapeless God,* ed. by H. J. Mooney, Jr. and T. F. Staley, pp. 91-115. See item 20.

604. Degnan, J. P. "J. F. Powers: Comic Satirist," *ColQ,* 16 (1968): 325-333.

605. Dolan, P. J. "God's Crooked Line: Powers' Morte d'Urban," *Renascence,* 21 (1969): 95-102.

606. Evans, F. ed. *J. F. Powers.* The Christian Critic Series. St. Louis, Missouri: B. Herder Book Company, n.d.

607. Green, M. B. "J. F. Powers and Catholic Writing," in *Yeats's Blessings on von Hügel,* pp. 97-127. See item 113.

608. Hagopian, J. V. "The Fathers of J. F. Powers," *SSF,* 5 (1968): 139-153.

609. Henault, M. J. and V. P. McCorry. "Morte D'Urban," *America,* 108 (1963): 290-294.

610. Kaufman, M. "J. F. Powers and Secularity," in *Adversity and Grace,* ed. by N. A. Scott, Jr., pp. 163-181. See item 28.

611. Malloy, Sister M. K. "The Catholic and Creativity: J. F. Powers," *ABR,* 15 (1964): 63-80.

612. Poss, S. "J. F. Powers: The Gin of Irony," *TCL,* 14 (1968): 65-74.

613. Scouffas, G. "J. F. Powers: On the Vitality of Disorder," *Crit,* 2, ii (1958): 41-58.

614. Sisk, J. P. "The Complex Moral Vision of J. F. Powers," *Crit,* 2, ii (1958): 28-40.

615. Steichen, D. M. "J. F. Powers and the Noonday Devil," *ABR,* 20 (1969): 528-551.

616. Vickery, J. B. "J. F. Powers' *Morte D'Urban:* Secularity and Grace," in *The Vision Obscured,* ed. by M. J. Friedman, pp. 45-65. See item 111.
    See also 83, 118, 288, 291, 294, 948, 1014.

JAMES PURDY

617. Burris, S. W. "The Emergency in Purdy's 'Daddy Wolfe'," *Renascence,* 20 (1968): 94-98.

618. Finklestein, S. "Acceptance of Alienation: John Updike and James Purdy," in *Existentialism and Alienation in American Literature.* See item 84.
   See also 1027.

THOMAS PYNCHON

619. Hunt, J. W. "Comic Escape and Anti-Vision: The Novels of Joseph Heller and Thomas Pynchon," in *Adversity and Grace,* ed. by N. A. Scott, Jr., pp. 87-111. See item 28.
   See also 177, 983, 1001.

PHILIP ROTH

620. Detweiler, R. *Four Spiritual Crises in Mid-Century American Fiction,* pp. 25-35. See item 8.

621. Leer, N. "Escape and Confrontation in the Short Stories of Philip Roth," *ChrS,* 49 (1966): 132-146.

622. Meeter, G. *Philip Roth/Bernard Malamud.* Contemporary Writers in Christian Perspective Series. Grand Rapids, Michigan: Wm. B. Eerdmans, 1968.
   See also 912.

J. D. SALINGER

623. Balke, B. T. "Some Judeo-Christian Themes Seen Through the Eyes of J. D. Salinger and Nathanael West," *Cresset,* 31 (1968): 14-18.

624. Barr, D. "Saints, Pilgrims and Artists," *Commonweal,* 67 (1957): 88-90. [Collected in *Salinger,* ed. by H. A. Grunwald. New York: Harper & Row, 1962, pp. 170-176.]

625. Detweiler, R. *Four Spiritual Crises in Mid-Century American Fiction,* pp. 36-43. See item 8.

626. Finklestein, S. "Cold War, Religious Revival and Family Alienation: William Styron, J. D. Salinger and Edward Albee," in *Existentialism and Alienation in American Literature.* See item 84.

627. Galloway, D. D. *The Absurd Hero in American Fiction: Updike, Styron, Bellow and Salinger.* See item 79.

628. Gwynn, F. L. and J. L. Blotner. The *Fiction of J. D. Salinger.* University of Pittsburgh Press, 1958. See esp. "IV. Seen through the Glass Family, Darkly: Religion through Satire,": 32-52.

629. Hamilton, K. *J. D. Salinger.* Contemporary Writers in Christian Perspective Series. Grand Rapids, Michigan: William B. Eerdmans, 1967.

630. Hamilton, K. "One Way to Use the Bible: The Example of J. D. Salinger," *ChrS*, 47 (1964): 243-251.

631. Jacobsen, J. "Beatific Signals: The Felicity of J. D. Salinger," *Commonweal*, 71 (1960): 589-591. [Collected in *Salinger*, ed. by H. A. Grunwald. New York: Harper & Row, 1962, pp. 165-170.]

632. Livingstone, J. T. "J. D. Salinger: The Artist's Struggle to Stand on Holy Ground," in *Adversity and Grace*, ed. by N. A. Scott, Jr., pp. 113-131. See item 28.

633. McIntyre, J. P. "A Preface for Franny and Zooey," *Critic*, 20 (1962): 25-28.

634. Miller, J. E. and A. Heiserman. "J. D. Salinger: Some Crazy Cliff," in *Quests Surd and Absurd*, by J. E. Miller, pp. 31-40. See item 82.

635. Panichas, G. A. "J. D. Salinger and the Russian Pilgrim," *GOTR*, 8 (1962-63): 111-126. [Collected in *Mansions of the Spirit*, ed. by G. A. Panichas, pp. 372-386. See item 770.]

636. "Religion and Esthetic Values," *Commonweal*, 71 (1959): 155-167. See especially "The Talent of J. D. Salinger."

637. Slabey, R. M. "*The Catcher in the Rye:* Christian Theme and Symbol," *CLAJ*, 6 (1963): 170-183.

638. Wakefield, D. "Salinger and the Search for Love," in *Salinger*, ed. by H. A. Grunwald, pp. 176-191. See item 631.

639. Wiegand, W. "Salinger and Kierkegaard," *MinnR*, 5 (1965): 137-156.
    See also 103, 105, 163, 282, 286, 289, 916, 984.

IGNAZIO SILONE

640. Gaffney, J. "Silone and the Pope," *Commonweal*, 89 (1968): 112-115.

641. Mueller, W. R. "The Theme of the Remnant: Ignazio Silone's *A Handful of Blackberries*," in *The Prophetic Voice in Modern Fiction*, pp. 158-183. See item 22.
    See also 19, 85, 271.

ISAAC BASHEVIS SINGER

642. Allentuck, M., ed. *The Achievement of Isaac Bashevis Singer.* Carbondale: Southern Illinois University Press, 1969.

643. Buchen, I. *Isaac Bashevis Singer and the Eternal Past.* New York: New York University Press, 1968.

644. Buchen, I. H. "Isaac Bashevis Singer and the Eternal Past," *Crit*, 8, iii (1966): 5-18.

645. Buchen, I. H. "Isaac Bashevis Singer and the Revival of Satan," *TSLL*, 9 (1967): 129-142.

646. Eisenberg, J. A. "Isaac Bashevis Singer—Passionate Primitive or Pious Puritan?" *Judaism*, 11 (1962): 345-356.

647. Fixler, M. "The Redeemers: Themes in the Fiction of Isaac Bashevis Singer," *KR*, 26 (1964): 371-386.

648. Howe, I. "I. B. Singer: False Messiahs and Modern Sensibility," in *Decline of the New*. New York: Harcourt, Brace and World Inc., c. 1963, pp.75-90.

649. Kahn, L. "Isaac Bashevis Singer," *Commonweal*, 81 (1965): 538-540.

650. Mucke, E. "Isaac B. Singer and Hassidic Philosophy," *MinnR*, 7 (1967): 214-221.

651. Newman, R. A. "Isaac Bashevis Singer," *HJ*, 65 (1966): 27-28.

652. Pondrom, C. N. "Isaac Bashevis Singer: An Interview," *ConL*, 10 (1969): 1-32 [Part I]. *ConL*, 10 (1970): 332-351 [Part II].

653. Siegel, B. "Sacred and Profane: Isaac Bashevis Singer's Embattled Spirits," *Crit*, 6, i (1963): 24-47.

654. Sloman, J. "Existentialism in Par Lagerkvist and Isaac Bashevis Singer," *MinnR*, 5 (1965): 206-212.

655. Wolkenfeld, J. S. "Isaac Bashevis Singer: The Faith of His Devils and Magicians," *Criticism*, 5 (1963): 349-359.

656. Zatlin, L. G. "The Themes of Isaac Bashevis Singer's Short Fiction," *Crit*, 11, ii (1969): 40-46.
See also 917.

MURIEL SPARK

657. Baldanza, F. "Muriel Spark and the Occult," *ConL*, 6 (1965): 190-203.

658. Dobie, A. B. "Muriel Spark's Definition of Reality," *Crit*, 12, i (1970): 20-27.

659. Greene, G. "Reading of Muriel Spark," *Thought*, 43 (1968): 393-407.

660. Grosskurth, P. "The World of Muriel Spark: Spirits or Spooks?" *TamR*, No. 39 (Spring 1966): 62-67.

661. Lodge, D. "The Uses and Abuses of Omniscience: Method and Meaning in Muriel Spark's *The Prime of Miss Jean Brodie*," *CritQ*, 12 (1970) : 235-257.

662. Malin, I. "The Deceptions of Muriel Spark," in *The Vision Obscured*, ed. by M. J. Friedman, pp. 95-107. See item 111.

663. Schneider, H. W. "A Writer in Her Prime: The Fiction of Muriel Spark," *Crit*, 5, ii (1962) : 28-45.

664. Spark, M. "My Conversion," *TC*, 170 (1961) : 58-63.

665. Wildman, J. H. "Translated by Muriel Spark," in *Nine Essays in Modern Literature*, ed. by D. E. Stanford. Baton Rouge: LSU Press, 1965, pp. 129-144.
See also 288, 933.

JOHN STEINBECK

666. Astro, R. "Steinbeck's Post-War Trilogy: A Return to Nature and the Natural Man," *TCL*, 16 (1970) : 109-122.

667. Cannon, G. "The Pauline Apostleship of Tom Joad," *CE*, 24 1962) : 222-224.

668. Crockett, H. K. "The Bible and the Grapes of Wrath," *CE*, 24 (1962) : 193-199.

669. Fontenrose, J. *John Steinbeck: An Introduction and Interpretation*. New York: Barnes & Noble, 1964.

670. Gordon, E. "The Winter of our Discontent," *PSB*, 55 (1962) : 44-47.

671. Jones, L. W. "The Whole Life and the Holy Life: John Steinbeck and the Riddle of Belief." *RIL*, 39 (1970) : 559-566.

672. Kennedy, J. S. "John Steinbeck: Life Affirmed and Dissolved," in *Fifty Years of the American Novel*, ed by H C. Gardiner, pp. 217-236. See item 170.

673. Morris, H. "*The Pearl:* Realism and Allegory," *EJ*, 52 (1963) : 487-495, 505.

674. Shockley, M. "Christian Symbolism in *The Grapes of Wrath*," *CE*, 18 (1956) : 87-90. Rebuttal: Carlson, E. W. "Rebuttal: "Symbolism in *The Grapes of Wrath*," *CE*, 19 (1958) : 172-175. Further comment, DeSchweinitz, G. "Steinbeck and Christianity," *CE*, 19 (1958) : 369.

675. Steinbeck, J. *Journal of a Novel; the East of Eden Letters*. New York: Viking Press, 1969. See especially pp. 90-91; 104-105; 107-108; 115-116; 128.
See also 48, 915, 938, 950.

WILLIAM STYRON

676. Bryant, J. H. "The Hopeful Stoicism of William Styron," *SAQ*, 62 (1963): 539-550.

677. Detweiler, R. *Four Spiritual Crises in Mid-Century American Fiction*, pp. 6-13. See item 8.

678. Drake, R. "Signs of the Times or Signs for All Times?" *ChrC*, 85 (1968): 1204-1206.

679. Finklestein, S. "Cold War, Religious Revival and Family Alienation: William Styron, J. D. Salinger and Edward Albee," in *Existentialism and Alienation in American Literature*. See item 84.

680. Fossum, R. H. *William Styron*. Contemporary Writers in Christian Perspective. Grand Rapids, Michigan: William B. Eerdmans, 1968.

681. Galloway, D. D. "The Absurd Man as a Tragic Hero: The Novels of William Styron," *TSLL* (1964): 512-534. [Also in *The Absurd Hero in American Fiction*, by D. D. Galloway. See item 79.]

682. Kaufmann, W. "Tragedy versus history: *The Confessions of Nat Turner*," in *Tragedy and Philosophy*, pp. 347-354. See item 270.

683. Lawson, L. "Cass Kinsolving: Kierkegaardian Man of Despair," *ConL*, 3 (1962): 54-66.

684. Stevenson, D. L. "Styron and the Fiction of the Fifties," *Crit*, 3, iii (1960): 47-58.

685. Urang, G. "Broader Vision: William Styron's *Set This House on Fire*," *Crit*, 8, ii (1965-66): 47-69.

686. Urang, G. "The Voices of Tragedy in the Novels of William Styron," in *Adversity and Grace*, ed. by N. A. Scott, Jr., pp. 183-209. See item 28.

687. Via, D. O., Jr. "Law and Grace in Styron's *Set This House on Fire*," *JR*, 51 (1971): 125-136.
See also 278, 282, 291, 298, 1009.

J. R. R. TOLKIEN

688. Barber, D. K. "The Meaning of *The Lord of the Rings*," *MankSE*, 2 (1967): 38-50.

689. Epstein, E. L. "The Novels of J. R. R. Tolkien and the Ethnology of Medieval Christendom," *PQ*, 48 (1969): 517-525.

690. Fuller, E. "The Lord of the Hobbits: J. R. R. Toikien," in *Tolkien and the Critics,* ed. by N. D. Isaacs and R. A. Zimbardo. Notre Dame, Indiana: University of Notre Dame Press, 1968, pp. 17-39.

691. Glover, W. B. "The Christian Character of Tolkien's Invented World," *Criticism,* 13 (1971): 39-53.

692. Miesel, S. "Some Religious Aspects of *Lord of the Rings,*" *RQ,* 3 (1968): 209-213.

693. Reilly, R. J. "Tolkien and the Fairy Story," *Thought,* 38 (1963): 89-106.

694. Spacks, P. M. "Ethical Patterns in *The Lord of the Rings,*" *Crit,* 3, i (1959): 30-42.
    See also 167, 168, 896, 1019.

JOHN UPDIKE

695. Detweiler, R. *Four Spiritual Crises in Mid-Century American Fiction,* pp. 14-24. See item 8.

696. Detweiler, R. "Updike's *Couples:* Eros Demythologized," *TCL,* 17 (1971): 235-246.

697. Finklestein, S. "Acceptance of Alienation: John Updike and James Purdy," in *Existentialism and Alienation in American Literature.* See item 84.

698. Galloway, D. D. "The Absurd Man as Saint: The Novels of John Updike," *MFS,* 10 (1964): 111-127. [Also in *The Absurd Hero in American Fiction,* by D. D. Galloway. See item 79.]

699. Hamilton, A. and K. *The Elements of John Updike.* Grand Rapids, Michigan: Wm. B. Eerdmans, 1970.

700. Hamilton, A. and K. *John Updike.* Contemporary Writers in Christian Perspective Series. Grand Rapids, Michigan: Wm. B. Eerdmans, 1967.

701. Hamilton, K. "John Updike: Chronicler of the Time of the Death of God," *ChrC,* 84 (1967): 745-748.

702. Hill, J. S. "Quest for Belief: Theme in the Novels of John Updike," *SHR,* 3 (1969): 166-175.

703. Kort, W. "John Updike's Fiction: Cross and Grace in *Beruf,*" *ATR,* 52 (1970): 151-167.

704. Myers, D. "The Questing Fear: Christian Allegory in John Updike's *The Centaur,*" *TCL,* 17 (1971): 73-81.

705. Novak, M. "Updike's Quest for Liturgy," *Commonweal,* 78 (1963): 192-195.

706. Rowland, S. J., Jr. "The Limits of Littleness," *ChrC,* 79 (1962): 840-841.

707. Standley, F. L. *"Rabbit, Run:* An Image of Life," *MQ,* 8 (1967): 371-386.

708. Stubbs, J. C. "Search for Perfection in *Rabbit, Run,"* *Crit,* 10, ii (1968): 94-101.

709. Yates, N. W. "The Doubt and Faith of John Updike," *CE,* 26 (1965): 469-474.
    See also 286, 291, 898, 921, 1018, 1028.

KURT VONNEGUT

710. Bodtke, R. "Great Sorrows, Small Joys: The World of Kurt Vonnegut, Jr.," *CrCur,* 20 (1970): 120-125.

711. May, J. R. "Vonnegut's Humor and the Limits of Hope," *TCL,* 18 (1972): 25-36.

712. Palmer, R. C. "Vonnegut's Major Concerns," *IEY,* 14 (1969): 3-10.

713. Ranly, E. W. "What Are People For?: Man, Fate and Kurt Vonnegut," *Commonweal,* 94 (1971): 207-211.
    See also 241, 954, 1001.

EDWARD LEWIS WALLANT

714. Ayo, N. "The Secular Heart: The Achievement of Edward Lewis Wallant," *Crit,* 12, ii (1970): 86-94.

715. Davis, W. V. "The Sound of Silence: Edward Lewis Wallant's *The Children at the Gate,"* *Cithara,* 8 (1968): 3-25.

716. Hutchison, R. S. "Plumber, Pawnbroker, and the Pursuit of Meaning," *ChrS,* 49 (1966): 245-254.
    See also 904, 937.

EVELYN WAUGH

717. Corr, P. "Evelyn Waugh: Sanity and Catholicism," *Studies,* 51 (1962): 388-399. [Reprinted in *CathM,* 61 (1963): 17-22.]

718. Cosman, M. "The Nature and Work of Evelyn Waugh," *ColQ,* 4 (1956): 428-441.

719. Davis, R. M. *Evelyn Waugh.* Christian Critic Series. St. Louis: B. Herder Book Company, n.d.

720. De Vitis, A. A. *Roman Holiday*[:] *The Catholic Novels of Evelyn Waugh.* New York: Bookman Associates, 1956.

721. Doyle, P. A. "The Church, History and Evelyn Waugh," *ABR*, 9 (1958-59): 202-208.

722. Doyle, P. A. *Evelyn Waugh.* Contemporary Writers in Christian Perspective Series. Grand Rapids, Michigan: William B. Eerdmans, 1969.

723. Grace, W. J. "Evelyn Waugh as a Social Critic," *Renascence*, 1 (1949): 28-40.

724. Hardy, J. E. *"Brideshead Revisited:* God, Man and Others," in *Man in the Modern Novel.* See item 212.

725. Hollis, C. *Evelyn Waugh,* revised edition. London: Longmans, Green and Company, 1958. See especially pp. 17-36.

726. Hynes, J. "Varieties of Death Wish: Evelyn Waugh's Central Theme," *Criticism*, 14 (1972): 65-77.

727. Ulanov, B. "The Ordeal of Evelyn Waugh," in *The Vision Obscured,* ed. by M. J. Friedman, pp. 79-93. See item 111.
    See also 118, 292, 295.

ELIE WIESEL

728. Friedman, M. "Elie Wiesel: The Modern Job," *Commonweal*, 85 (1966): 48-52.

729. Halperin, I. "Postscript to Death," *Commonweal*, 79 (1964): 713-715.

730. Leviant, C. "Elie Wiesel: A Soul on Fire," *SatR*, 53 (Jan. 31, 1970): 25-28.

731. Sherwin, B. L. "Elie Wiesel and Jewish Theology," *Judaism*, 18 (1969): 39-52.
    See also 929.

RICHARD WRIGHT

732. Lawson, L. "Cross Damon: Kierkegaardian Man of Dread," *CLAJ*, 14 (1971): 298-316.

733. Scott, N. A., Jr. "The Dark and Haunted Tower of Richard Wright," in *Five Black Writers,* ed. by D. B. Gibson. New York University Press, 1970, pp. 12-25.

734. Scott, N. A., Jr. "The Search for Beliefs in the Fiction of Richard Wright," *UR*, 23 (1956) and (1957): 19-24 and 131-138.

II. RELIGION, LITERATURE AND THE ARTS: MATERIALS RELATING TO THE STUDY OF RELIGION AND FICTION

II. RELIGION, LITERATURE AND THE ARTS: MATERIALS RELATING TO THE STUDY OF RELIGION AND FICTION

A. General Critical Studies

735. Auerbach, E. *Mimesis: The Representation of Reality in Western Literature.* Tr. by W. R. Trask. Garden City, New York: Doubleday, 1957. First published, 1946.

736. Babbage, S. B. "Christianity and Literature," *CTSB,* 60 (July 1967): 31-42.

737. Barth, J. R. "Theology and Modern Literature," *America,* 104 (1961): 626-630.

738. Cahill, D. J. "Theology and Literature: A Modern Movement," *Response,* 10 (1968-69): 69-73.

739. Callahan, D. J. "Literature and Doctrine," *Commonweal,* 69 (1958): 96-98.

740. DeRougemont, D. *Love in the Western World,* revised edition. Garden City: Doubleday, 1957.

741. Detweiler, R. "Religion as a Humanizing Force in Literature" [part of a symposium: "Religion as a Humanizing Force in Man's History"], *SHR*, 4 (1970): 201-206.

742. Driver, T. F. "The Study of Religion and Literature: Siblings in the Academic House," in *The Study of Religion in Colleges and Universities*, ed. by P. Ramsey and J. F. Wilson. Princeton, N.J.: Princeton University Press, 1970, pp. 304-329.

743. Elmen, P. "Holiness and the Literary Mind," *ChrC*, 78 (1961): 232-233.

744. Farrer, A. *The Glass of Vision*. London: Dacre, 1948.

745. Gallagher, M. P. "Human Values in Modern Literature," *Studies*, 57 (1968): 142-153.

746. Gardner, H. *Religion and Literature*. New York: Oxford University Press, 1971.

747. Glicksberg, C. I. *Literature and Religion: A Study in Conflict*. Dallas: SMU Press, 1960.

748. Glicksberg, C. I. "The Religious Revival in Contemporary Literature," *WHR*, 11 (1957): 65-78.

749. Gunn, G. B. "Literature and its Relation to Religion," *JR*, 50 (1970): 268-291.

750. Gunn, G. B., ed. *Literature and Religion*. Harper Forum Books, 1971.

751. Hanna, T. L. "A Question: What Does One Mean by Religious Literature?" *CLS*, 2 (1965): 375-385. [Collected in *Mansions of the Spirit*, ed. by G. A. Panichas, pp. 74-86. See item 770.]

752. Herberg, W. "Religion and the Work of Literature," *L&RN*, 1 (1960): 3-7.

753. Hoffman, F. J. "The Religious Crisis in Modern Literature," *CLS*, 3 (1966): 263-272.

754. Hopper, S. R. "Reports and Prophecies in the Literature of Our Time," *ChrS*, 40 (1957): 312-330.

755. Hopper, S. R. *Spiritual Problems in Contemporary Literature*. Harper Torchbooks, The Cloister Library, 1957. First printed, Harper, 1952.

756. Hunt, J. W. "The Artist and the Church: Who Speaks? Who Listens?", *Encounter*, 26 (1965): 506-513.

757. Huttar, C. A. *Imagination and the Spirit*. Grand Rapids, Michigan: Wm. B. Eerdmans Publishing Company, 1971.

758. Jarrett-Kerr, M. *Studies in Literature and Belief.* London: Rockcliff, 1954.

759. Kaufmann, W. *Religion from Tolstoy to Camus.* New York: Harper and Row, 1961.

760. Killinger, J. *The Failure of Theology in Modern Literature.* New York-Nashville: Abingdon Press, 1963.

761. Krumm, J. Mc. "Theology and Literature: The Terms of the Dialogue on the Modern Scene," in *The Climate of Faith in Modern Literature,* ed. by N. A. Scott, Jr., pp. 19-41. See item 851.

762. Lawler, J. G. *The Christian Image.* Pittsburgh: Duquesne University Press, 1966.

763. Lee, R. J. "On the Study of Literature and Theology," *Response,* 10 (1968-69): 59-68.

764. Lewis, R. W. B. "Hold on Hard to the Huckleberry Bushes," *SR,* 67 (1959): 462-477. [Collected in *Literature and Religion,* ed. by G. B. Gunn, pp. 87-101. See item 750.]

765. Lynch, W. F. *Christ and Apollo: The Dimensions of the Literary Imagination.* New York: Sheed and Ward, 1960.

766. Miller, J. H. "Literature and Religion," in *Relations of Literary Study: Essays on Interdisciplinary Contributions,* ed. by J. Thorpe. New York: Modern Language Association of America, 1967, pp. 111-126.

767. Newport, J. P. *Theology and Contemporary Art Forms.* Waco, Texas: Word Books, 1971. See especially Part II: 32-42.

768. O'Connor, W. V., ed. *Religion in American Literature.* Seattle: University of Washington Press, 1967.

769. Ong, W. J. *The Barbarian Within.* New York: Macmillan Company, 1962. See especially part one, "Words are More than Things": 15-145.

770. Panichas, G. A., ed. *Mansions of the Spirit: Essays on Literature and Religion.* New York: Hawthorn Books, Inc., 1967.

771. Peyre, H. "Religion and Literary Scholarship in France," *PMLA,* 77 (Part 1) (1962): 345-363.

772. Pitt, V. *The Writer and the Modern World[:] A Study in Literature and Dogma.* London: *SPCK,* 1966.

773. Robbins, D. "Religion and Literature: An Overview," *ATR,* 50 (1968): 283-307.

774. Roth, L. "Religion and Literature," *HJ*, 60 (1961) : 24-34.

775. Scott, N. A., Jr. "Beneath the Hammer of Truth," *C&C*, 16 (1956) : 124-126.

776. Scott, N. A., Jr. *The Broken Center: Studies in the Theological Horizon of Modern Literature.* New Haven: Yale University Press, 1966.

777. Scott, N. A., Jr. "The 'Conscience' of the New Literature," in *The Shaken Realist; Essays in Modern Literature in Honor of Frederick J. Hoffman,* ed. by M. J. Friedman and J. B. Vickery. Baton Rouge: Louisiana State University Press, 1970, pp. 251-283.

778. Scott, N. A., Jr. *Modern Literature and the Religious Frontier.* New York: Harper & Bros., 1958.

779. Scott, N. A., Jr. *Negative Capability: Studies in the New Literature and the Religious Situation.* New Haven: Yale University Press, 1969.

780. Scott, N. A., Jr. "Poetry and Prayer," *Thought,* 41 (1966) : 61-80. [Collected in *Literature and Religion,* ed. by G. B. Gunn, pp. 191-210. See item 750.]

781. Shumaker, W. *Literature and the Irrational[:] A Study in Anthropological Backgrounds.* New York: Washington Square Press, 1966. C. 1960 by Prentice-Hall, Inc.

782. Stewart, R. *American Literature and Christian Doctrine.* Baton Rouge: LSU Press, 1958.

783. Stewart, R. "American Literature and the Christian Tradition," published as a "Faculty Paper" by the National Council of the Episcopal Church, 1955.

784. TeSelle, S. Mc. "What is Religion in Literature?" *America,* 119 (1968) : 614-617.

785. Thorson, G. "The Religious Significance of Modern Literature," *Response,* 2 (1960) : 17-24.

786. Turnell, M. *Modern Literature and Christian Faith.* Westminster, Maryland: The Newman Press, 1961.

787. Walsh, C. "A Hope for Literature," in *The Climate of Faith in Modern Literature,* ed. by N. A. Scott, Jr., pp. 207-233. See item 851.

788. Wienhorst, S. "Theological Responses to Modern Literature: A Methodological Inquiry," *Cresset,* 26 (1963) : 8-14.

789. Wilder, A. N. *The New Voice: Religion, Literature, Hermeneutics.* New York: Herder & Herder, 1969.
     See also 88, 180, 287, 860, 880, 925, 942, 958, 959, 972, 973, 974, 996, 1004, 1005, 1026.

B. Religion and Aesthetics

790. Arseniev, N. S. "The Religious Meaning of the Experience of Beauty," *CLS,* 2 (1965): 315-322.

791. Burkeley, F. J. "Importance of a Christian Aesthetic in Catholic Life," *NSch,* 20 (1946): 126-156.

792. Jenkinson, R. W. "Towards a Christian Aesthetic," *DownR,* 67, no. 207 (1948-49): 49-61.

793. Maritain, J. *Creative Intuition in Art and Poetry.* New York: Pantheon Books, Inc., 1953.

794. Murchland, B. G. "Theology and Literature," *Commonweal,* 71 (1959): 63-66.

795. "Religion and Esthetic Values," *Commonweal,* 71 (1959): 155-167.

796. Rey, W. H. "Theological Aesthetics?" *GR,* 35 (1960): 243-261.

797. Sayers, D. L. "Towards a Christian Aesthetic," in *Unpopular Opinions: Twenty-one Essays.* New York: Harcourt, Brace & Company, 1947, pp. 30-47.

798. Scott, N. A., Jr. "Maritain in His Role as Aesthetician," *RevM,* 8 (1955): 480-492.
     See also 807, 854, 864.

C. Religion and the Arts

799. Driver, T. F. "The Arts and the Christian Evangel," *ChrS,* 40 (1957): 331-337.

800. Eversole, F., ed. *Christian Faith and the Contemporary Arts.* Nashville: Abingdon Press, 1962.

801. Garvin, H. R. "Religion and the Arts: The Coming Dangers," *ChrS,* 42 (1959): 275-283.

802. Harned, D. B. *Theology and the Arts.* Philadelphia: The Westminster Press, 1966.

803. Hazelton, R. *A Theological Approach to Art.* Nashville & New York: Abingdon, 1967.

804. Jarrett-Kerr, M. "The 491 Pitfalls of the Christian Artist," in *The Climate of Faith in Modern Literature,* ed. by N. A. Scott, Jr., pp. 177-206. See item 851.

805. Leeuw, G. van der. *Sacred and Profane Beauty: The Holy in Art.* Tr. by D. E. Green. New York: Holt, Rinehart and Winston, 1963.

806. Martin, F. D. *Art and the Religious Experience*[:] *The "Language" of the Sacred.* Cranbury, N.J.: Bucknell University Press, 1972.

807. Pittenger, W. N. "Art and the Christian," *ChrC,* 64 (1947): 1612-1615.

808. Wilder, A. N. "Art and Theological Meaning," *USQR,* 17 (1962): 37-47.

809. Wilder, A. N. "Christianity and the Arts: The Historic Divorce and the Contemporary Situation," *ChrS,* 40 (1957): 261-268.

810. Wilder, A. N. "The Church's New Concern with the Arts," *C&C,* 17 (1957): 12-14.
  See also 217, 899, 992, 993.

D. Religion and Literary Criticism

811. Anonymous. "How Autonomous is Art?" *ChrC,* 82 (1965): 635-636.

812. Austin, A. "Problem of Poetry and Belief," *UR,* 27 (1961): 197-202.

813. Austin, A. "T. S. Eliot's Quandary," *UR,* 27 (1960): 143-148.

814. Battenhouse, R. W. "The Relation of Theology to Literary Criticism," *JB&R,* 13 (1945): 16-22.

815. Bedell, G. C. "The Technique of Fiction Revisited," *ATR,* 50 (1968): 275-282.

816. Bethell, S. L. *Literary Criticism.* London: Dennis Dobson Ltd., 1948.

817. Blehl, V. F. "Literature and Religious Belief," *CLS,* 2 (1965): 303-314. [Collected in *Mansions of the Spirit,* ed. by G. A. Panichas, pp. 105-120. See item 770.]

818. Bloom, E. A. "The Vatic Temper in Literary Criticism," *Criticism*, 5 (1963): 297-315.

819. Buckley, V. "Criticism and Theological Standards," in *The New Orpheus*, ed. by N. A. Scott, Jr., pp. 172-186. See item 856.

820. Buckley, V. *Poetry and Morality: Studies on the Criticism of Matthew Arnold, T. S. Eliot and F. R. Leavis*. London: Chatto and Windus, 1959.

821. Cary, N. R. "An Apologetic for Christian Criticism: A Comment on 'The Vatic Temper in Literary Criticism'," *Criticism*, 6 (1964): 266-272. Reply by Edward Bloom, pp. 273-274.

822. Connolly, F. X. "Is a Christian Theory of Literature Possible?" *The McAuley Lectures*, 1961. West Hartford, Connecticut: St. Joseph College, 1962, pp. 31-48.

823. Connolly, F. X. "Literary Consciousness and the Literary Conscience," *Thought*, 25 (1950): 663-680.

824. Daub, O. C. "Dialog: Christian Criticism is not . . . " *NCCL*, 17, i (1967): 13-15.

825. Dixon, J. W. "The Ontological Intransigence of the Aesthetic Fact," *CLS*, 3 (1966): 247-257.

826. Donahue, C. "Literary Criticism and Philosophy," *Thought*, 26 (1951-52): 501-511.

827. Eliot, T. S. "Religion and Literature," in *The New Orpheus*, ed. by N. A. Scott, Jr., pp. 223-235. See item 856.

828. Fitch, R. E. "The Christian Criticism of Literature," *C&C*, 17 (1957): 52-54. Response by T. F. Driver, "Literary Criticism and the Christian Conscience: A Reply to Mr. Fitch," 17 (1957): 91-94.

829. Frye, N. *Anatomy of Criticism*. Princeton University Press, 1957.

830. Frye, R. M. "A Christian Approach to Literature," *ChrS*, 37 (1954): 505-514.

831. Frye, R. M. *Perspective on Man: Literature and the Christian Tradition*. Philadelphia: The Westminster Press, 1961.

832. Gardiner, H. C. *Norms for the Novel*, revised edition. Garden City, New York: Hanover House (Division of Doubleday), 1960.

833. Gardner, H. *The Business of Criticism*. London: Oxford University Press, 1959.

834. Gregor, I. "Towards a Christian Literary Criticism," *Month,* 33 n.s. (1965): 239-249.

835. Hassan, I. H. "Beyond a Theory of Literature: Intimations of Apocalypse?" in *Comparative Literature: Matter and Method,* ed. by A. O. Aldridge, pp. 25-35. See item 65.

836. Hazo, S. J. "Belief and the Critic," *Renascence,* 13 (1961): 187-199.

837. Jackson, R. S.; J. Sittler; E. A. Bloom. "A Symposium: Is a Christian Literary Criticism Possible and Desirable?", *L&RN,* 1 (1960): 21-28.

838. James, G. I. "Autonomy of the Work of Art: Modern Criticism and the Christian Tradition," *SR,* 70 (1962): 296-318. [Collected in *The New Orpheus,* ed. by N. A. Scott, Jr., pp. 187-209. See item 856.]

839. Kelly, J. J. "Catholic Literary Criticism: Some Current Implications," *Critic,* 21 (1962): 49-52.

840. Krieger, M. "Recent Criticism, Thematics, and Existentialist Dilemma," *CentR,* 4 (1960): 32-50.

841. McDonald, W. E. "The Literary Criticism of Amos Wilder," *Soundings,* 52 (1969): 99-109.

842. McDonnell, T. P. "Criticism and Belief: The Life of the Catholic Critic," *Renascence,* 11 (1959): 59-64.

843. May, J. R. "Language-Event as Promise: Reflections on Theology and Literature," *CJT,* 16 (1970): 129-139.

844. Noel, D. C. "Nathan Scott and the Nostalgic Fallacy: A Close Reading of Theological Criticism," *JAAR,* 38 (1970): 347-366. Rejoinder by Mr. Scott, "On the Fallacies of a 'Close Reader'," *JAAR,* 39 (1971): 76-82. Further rejoinder by Mr. Noel, *JAAR,* 39 (1971): 198-199.

845. Nott, K. *The Emperor's Clothes.* Bloomington: Indiana University Press, 1958.

846. Ong, W. J. "The Jinnee in the Well-Wrought Urn," in *The New Orpheus,* ed. by N. A. Scott, Jr., pp. 210-221. See item 856.

847. Panichas, G. A. "Introduction: Mansions of the Spirit," *CLS,* 2 (1965): 289-292.

848. Reist, J. S., Jr. "The Lost Harmony: A Study of Methodology for Theological Literary Criticism," *ATR,* 53 (1971): 174-186.

849. Reist, J. S., Jr. "What doth thou in this world? A Study of Christological Possibilities in Modern Literature," *Foun*, 11 (1968): 68-87.

850. Ruland, V. "Literary Critics and Theologians," *America*, 119 (1968): 618-620.

851. Scott, N. A., Jr., ed. *The Climate of Faith in Modern Literature.* New York: Seabury Press, 1964.

852. Scott, N. A., Jr. "The Collaboration of Vision in the Poetic Act," *ChrS*, 40 (1957): 277-295. [Also in *CrCur*, 7 (1957): 137-153.]

853. Scott, N. A., Jr. "Criticism and the Religious Horizon," in *Religion and the Arts Tomorrow*, ed. by H. Hunter. New York: Holt, Rinehart and Winston, Inc., 1971.

854. Scott, N. A., Jr. "Faith and Art in a World Awry," in *The Climate of Faith in Modern Literature*, ed. by N. A. Scott, Jr., pp. 3-18. See item 851.

855. Scott, N. A., Jr. "The Modern Experiment in Criticism: A Theological Appraisal," in *The New Orpheus*, pp. 141-171. See item 856.

856. Scott, N. A., Jr., ed. *The New Orpheus: Essays Toward a Christian Poetic.* New York: Sheed & Ward, 1964.

857. Scott, N. A., Jr. "The Relation of Theology to Literary Criticism," *JR*, 33 (1953): 266-277.

858. Spanos, W. V. "The Critical Imperatives of Alienation: The Theological Perspective of Nathan Scott's Literary Criticism," *JR*, 48 (1968): 89-103.

859. Spanos, W. V. "Theological Criticism," *ConL*, 9 (1968): 246-250.

860. Stein, W. *Criticism as Dialogue.* Cambridge at the University Press, 1969.

861. Stewart, D. H. "Myth and Truth in Criticism," *MinnR*, 3 (1963): 452-460.

862. Summers, J. H. "Christian Literary Scholars," *ChrS*, 47 (1964): 94-99.

863. Tate, A. "Orthodoxy and the Standard of Literature," *New Repub*, 128 (Jan. 5, 1953): 24-25.

864. TeSelle, S. Mc. *Literature and the Christian Life.* New Haven and London: Yale University Press, 1966.

865. Vahanian, G. *Wait Without Idols.* New York: G. Braziller, 1964.

866. Via, D. O., Jr. "Sense of Presence." *JR*, 51 (1971): 57-66.

867. Waggoner, H. H. " 'Point of View' in American Literary Scholar-ship and Criticism," *CLS*, 2 (1965): 293-302. [Collected in *Mansions of the Spirit*, ed. by G. A. Panichas, pp. 47-58. See item 770.]

868. Weatherby, H. L. "Two Medievalists: Lewis and Eliot on Chris-tianity and Literature," *SR*, 78 (1970): 330-347.

869. Wilder, A. "Anterooms of Faith?", *New Repub*, 141 (September 14, 1959): 16-18.

870. Wilder, A. N. *Theology and Modern Literature.* Cambridge, Massachusetts: Harvard University Press [c. 1958].

871. Wilder, A. N. "The Uses of a Theological Criticism," *Soundings*, 52 (1969): 84-98. [Collected in *Literature and Religion*, ed. by G. B. Gunn, pp. 37-52. See item 750.]

872. Wilson, C. "The Need for an Existential Criticism," in *The Strength to Dream*, pp. 207-211. See item 884.

873. Wimsatt, W. K., Jr. "Poetry and Christian Thinking," *Thought*, 26 (1951): 219-232.
      See also 55, 226, 770, 789, 882, 963, 967, 985, 1008.

E. Religion and the Literary Imagination

874. Driver, T. F. "Latent Image: Literary Sources of Theological Understanding," *USQR*, 23 (1968): 169-181.

875. Hart, J. "Christ and Apollo: The Modern Debate," *Renascence*, 16 (1964): 95-102.

876. Lynch, W. F. "The Theological Imagination," in *The New Or-pheus*, ed. by N. A. Scott, Jr., pp. 115-138. See item 856. This essay is from Father Lynch's book, *Christ and Apollo*, Sheed & Ward, 1960.

877. Lynch, W. F. "Theology and the Imagination I," *Thought*, 29 (1954): 61-86.

878. Lynch, W. F. "Theology and the Imagination II: The Evocative Symbol," *Thought*, 29 (1954): 529-554.

879. Merchant, W. M. "Christianity and the Modern Literary Imagination: A Survey of Allegiances," in *The Climate of Faith in Modern Literature*, ed. by N. A. Scott, Jr., pp. 42-64. See item 851.

880. Scott, N. A. "The Broken Center: A Definition of the Crisis of Values in Modern Literature," in *Symbolism in Religion and Literature*, ed. by R. May. New York: G. Braziller [c. 1960], pp. 178-202. [Also collected in *Society and Self*, ed. by Bartlett H. Stoodley. The Free Press of Glencoe, 1962, pp. 599-617.]

881. Scott, N. A., Jr. "Introduction: Theology and the Literary Imagination," in *Adversity and Grace*, pp. 1-26. See item 28.

882. Scott, N. A., Jr. "Prolegomenon to a Christian Poetic," *JR*, 35 (1955): 191-206.

883. Scott, N. A., Jr. *The Wild Prayer of Longing[:] Poetry and the Sacred*. New Haven & London: Yale University Press, 1971.

884. Wilson, C. *The Strength to Dream[:] Literature and the Imagination*. Boston: Houghton Mifflin Co., 1962.
    See also 757, 765, 852, 987, 1004.

III. EARLIER BIBLIOGRAPHIES ON RELIGION AND LITERATURE

III. EARLIER BIBLIOGRAPHIES ON RELIGION AND LITERATURE

885. Bryer, J. R., ed. *Fifteen Modern American Authors: A Survey of Research and Criticism.* Durham, N.C.: Duke University Press, 1969. See especially "William Faulkner": 175-210; "Ernest Hemingway": 275-300; "John Steinbeck": 369-388.

886. Burr, N. R. *A Critical Bibliography of Religion in America,* Parts 3, 4 and 5. Princeton, N.J.: Princeton University Press, 1961. See Part 4, "Religion in the Arts and Literature, Religion and the Arts": 756-953; especially "Religion and Literature": 851-859 and "Fiction": 880-909.

887. Cary, N. and A. Casselman. "Bibliography of Religion and Literature," *Universitas,* 2 (1964): 120-128.

888. Deffner, D. L. "Theology and Modern Literature—Survey," *CTM,* 36 (1965): 706-720.

889. Driver, T. F. "Christianity and the Arts: Religion and Literature," *USQR,* 15 (1960): 142-150.

890. Frampton, M. "Religion and the Modern Novel," in *The Shapeless God,* ed. by H. J. Mooney and T. F. Staley, pp. 207-217. See item 20.

891. Griffin, E. G. *Bibliography of Literature and Religion.* University of Alberta, Department of English, March, 1969.

892. Lehan, R. "French and American Philosophical and Literary Existentialism; A Selected Checklist," *ConL,* 1 (1960) : 74-88.

893. Scott, N. A., Jr. "Religion and Literature: A Selected Bibliography," *ChrS,* 41 (1958) : 70-76.

894. Vos, N. "A Bibliography of Bibliographies on Christianity and Literature," and "Selective Bibliography of Books on Christianity and Literature," *NCCL,* 21, i/ii (1971-72) : 11-26.

895. Wheeler, B. "Religious Themes in Contemporary Literature; an introductory bibliography," *JB&R,* 27 (1959) : 50-56. Updates: 32 (1964) : 50; 32 (1964) : 133.

APPENDICES

Appendix I

ARTICLES RECORDED BETWEEN TIME OF
COMPILATION AND TIME OF PUBLICATION

896. Auden, W. H. "Good and Evil in *The Lord of the Rings,*" *CritQ,*
10 (1968): 138-142.

897. Bedell, G. C. *Kierkegaard and Faulkner: Modalities of Existence.*
Baton Rouge: LSU Press, 1972.

898. Burchard, R. C. *John Updike: Yea Savings.* Carbondale & Edwardsville, Illinois: Southern Illinois University Press, 1971.

899. Burgess, A. "Religion and the Arts: I. The Manicheans," *TLS,*
65 (3 March, 1966): 153-154.

900. Cahill, D. J. "Jerzy Kosinski: Retreat from Violence," *TCL,* 18
(1972): 121-132.

901. Cansler, R. L. "Stranger in a Strange Land: Science Fiction as
Literature of Creative Imagination, Social Criticism, and En-
tertainment," *Journal of Popular Culture,* 5 (1972): 944-954.

902. Chilson, R. W. "The Christ of Nikos Kazantzakis," *Thought,* 47
(1972): 69-89.

903. Coulthard, A. R. "Graham Greene's 'The Hint of an Explanation': A Reinterpretation," *SSF*, 8 (1971): 601-605.

904. Davis, W. V. "The Renewal of Dialogic Immediacy in Edward Lewis Wallant," *Renascence*, 24 (1972): 59-69.

905. Detweiler, R. "The Moment of Death in Modern Fiction," *ConL*, 13 (1972): 269-294.

906. D'meo, S. "Man and Apollo: A Look at Religion in the Science Fantasies of Ray Bradbury," *Journal of Popular Culture*, 5 (1972): 970-978.

907. Dowie, W. "Walker Percy: Sensualist-Thinker," *Novel*, 6 (1972): 52-65.

908. Driskell, L. V. & J. T. Brittain. *The Eternal Crossroads: The Art of Flannery O'Connor*. Lexington, Kentucky: University Press of Kentucky, 1971.

909. Eggenschwiler, D. *The Christian Humanism of Flannery O'Connor*. Detroit: Wayne State University Press, 1972.

910. Feeley, K. *Flannery O'Connor: The Voice of the Peacock*. New Brunswick, N.J.: Rutgers University Press, 1972.

911. Ficken, C. "The Christ Story in *A Fable*," *MissQ*, 23 (1970): 251-264.

912. Friedman, A. W. "The Jew's Complaint in Recent American Fiction: Beyond Exodus and Still in the Wilderness," *SoR*, 8 n.s. (1972): 41-59.

913. Glicksberg, C. I. "The Literature of Silence," *CentR*, 14 (1970): 166-176.

914. Glicksberg, C. I. "The Lost Self in Modern Literature," *Person*, 53 (1962): 527-538.

915. Goldhurst, W. "*Of Mice and Men:* John Steinbeck's Parable of The Curse of Cain," *Western American Literature*, 6 (1971): 123-135.

916. Goldstein, B. & S. "Ego and 'Hapworth'," *Renascence*, 24 (1972): 159-167. [Salinger]

917. Gottlieb, E. "Singer and Hawthorne: A Prevalence of Satan," *SoR*, 8 n.s. (1972): 359-370.

918. Grant, W. E. "Benjy's Branch: Symbolic Method in Part I of *The Sound and the Fury*," *TSLL*, 13 (1972): 705-710.

919. Guers-Villate, Y. "Revolt and Submission in Camus and Bernanos," *Renascence*, 24 (1972): 189-197.

920. Hamilton, A. "Loneliness and Alienation: The Life and Work of Carson McCullers," *DR*, 50 (1970): 215-229.

921. Hamilton, A. and K. "John Updike's Prescription for Survival," *ChrC*, 89 (1972): 740-744.

922. Hamiiton, J. B. "Hemingway and the Christian Paradox," *Renascence*, 2 (1972): 141-154.

923. Hamilton, K. "Comedy in a Theological Perspective," *RIL*, 41 (1972): 222-232.

924. Hamilton, K. and R. T. Haverluck. "Laughter and Vision," *Soundings*, 55 (1972): 163-177.

925. Hopper, S. R. and D. L. Miller, eds. *Interpretation: The Poetry of Meaning: Philosophical, Religious and Literary Inquiries into the Expression of Human Experience Through Language.* New York: Harcourt Brace, 1972.

926. Howell, E. "Flannery O'Connor and the Home Country," *Renascence*, 24 (1972): 171-176.

927. Hynes, J. "Percy's Reliques," *CrCur*, 22 (1972): 117-120, 128.

928. Hynes, J. "The 'Facts' at *The Heart of the Matter*," *TSLL*, 13 (1972): 711-726.

929. Idinopulos, T. A. "The Holocaust in the Stories of Elie Wiesel," *Soundings*, 55 (1972): 200-215.

930. Keller, J. C. "The Figures of the Empiricist and the Rationalist in the Fiction of Flannery O'Connor," *ArQ*, 28 (1972): 263-273.

931. Kropf, C. R. "Theme and Setting in 'A Good Man Is Hard to Find'," *Renascence*, 24 (1972): 177-180.

932. Kulshrestha, C. "A Conversation with Saul Bellow," *ChiR*, 23, iv and 24, i [double issue] (n.d.): 7-15.

933. Laffin, G. S. "Muriel Spark's Portrait of the Artist as a Young Girl," *Renascence*, 24 (1972): 213-223.

934. Lale, M. and J. Williams. "The Narrator of *The Painted Bird*: A Case Study," *Renascence*, 24 (1972): 198-206. [Jerzy Kosinski]

935. Lebowitz, N. *Humanism and the Absurd in the Modern Novel.* Evanston: Northwestern University Press, 1971.

936. LeClair, T. "Essential Opposition: the Novels of Anthony Burgess," *Crit*, 12, iii (1971): 77-94.

937. Lewis, R. W. "The Hung-Up Heroes of Edward Lewis Wallant,"
      Renascence, 24 (1972) : 70-84.

938. Lieber, T. M. "Talismanic Patterns in the Novels of John Stein-
      beck," *AL,* 44 (1972) : 262-275.

939. Livingston, H. "Religious Intrusion in Hemingway's *The Killers,"
      English Record,* 21, iii (1971) : 42-44.

940. McInerny, R. "The Greene-ing of America," *Commonweal,* 95
      (Oct. 15, 1972) : 59-61.

941. May, J. R. "The Apprenticeship of a Catholic Writer: Mauriac,"
      Renascence, 24 (1972) : 181-188.

942. May, J. R. "Of Huckleberry Bushes and the New Hermeneutic,"
      Renascence, 24 (1972) : 85-95.

943. May, J. R. *Toward a New Earth: Apocalypse in the American
      Novel.* Notre Dame: University of Notre Dame Press, 1972.

944. Montgomery, M. "A Note on Flannery O'Connor's Terrible and
      Violent Prophecy of Mercy," *ForumH,* 7, iii (1969) : 4-7.

945. Montgomery, M. "Flannery O'Connor's Transformation of the
      Sentimental," *MissQ,* 25 (1971-72) : 1-18.

946. Muller, G. *Nightmares and Visions: Flannery O'Connor and the
      Catholic Grotesque.* Athens: University of Georgia Press, 1971.

947. Pfeiffer, J. R. *"Katz und Maus* [*Cat and Mouse*]: Grass's Debt to
      Augustine," *PLL,* 7 (1971) : 279-292.

948. Phelps, D. "Reasonable, Holy and Living," *MinnR,* 9 (1969) :
      57-62. [J. F. Powers]

949. Pinsker, S. *The Schlemiel as Metaphor: Studies in the Yiddish
      and American Jewish Novel.* Carbondale: Southern Illinois
      University Press, 1971.

950. Pratt, J. C. *John Steinbeck.* Contemporary Authors in Christian
      Perspective Series. Grand Rapids, Michigan: Wm. B. Eerd-
      mans, 1970.

951. Pritchard, W. H. "The Novels of Anthony Burgess," *MR,* 7
      (1966) : 525-539.

952. Rees, R. A. "Toward a Bibliography of the Bible in American
      Literature," *BB,* 29 (1972) : 101-108.

953. Rose, A. H. "Sin and the City: The Uses of Disorder in the
      Urban Novel," *CentR,* 16 (1972) : 203-220.

954. Schulz, M. "The Unconfirmed Thesis: Kurt Vonnegut, Black Humor, and Contemporary Art," *Crit,* 12, iii (1970): 5-28.

955. Sonnenfeld, A. "Flannery O'Connor: The Catholic Writer as Baptist," *ConL,* 13 (1972): 445-457.

956. Sternlicht, S. "Prologue to the Sad Comedies: Graham Greene's Major Early Novels," *MQ,* 12 (1971): 427-435.

957. Tarbox, R. "Eudora Welty's Fiction: The Salvation Theme," *AI,* 29 (1972): 70-91.

958. Van Der Weele, S. J. "Some Data on the Origins of the Modern Concern with the Relationship between Theology and Literature," *NCCL,* 20, iv (1971): 8-11.

959. Van Kaam, A. L. & K. Healy. *The Demon and the Dove; Personality Growth Through Literature.* Pittsburgh: Duquesne University Press, 1967. [Camus, G. Greene]

960 Vos, N. "Space as Metaphor: The Hole, the Wall, and the Arch," *Reformed Journal,* 21 (November 1971): 7-9.

961. Webster, H. C. *After the Trauma: Representative British Novelists Since 1920.* Lexington: The University Press of Kentucky, 1970. [E. Waugh, G. Greene, J. Cary, *et al.*]

962. Ziolkowski, T. *Fictional Transfigurations of Jesus.* Princeton, N.J.: Princeton University Press, 1972.

Appendix II

963. Altieri, C. F. "Northrop Frye and the Problem of Spiritual Authority," *PMLA,* 87 (1972): 964-975.

964. Altizer, T. J. J. "The Religious Meaning of Myth and Symbol," in *Truth, Myth, and Symbol,* ed. by T. J. J. Altizer, W. Beardslee, J. H. Young. Englewood Cliffs, N.J.: Prentice-Hall, Inc. 1962: pp. 87-108.

965. Atkins, A. "Caprice: The Myth of the Fall in Anselm and Dostoevsky," *JR,* 47 (1967): 295-312.

966. Atkins, A. "Fate and Freedom: Camus' *The Stranger,*" *Renascence,* 21 (1969): 64-75, 110.

967. Atkins, A. "If Theology Were Hypothetical," *CrCur,* 18 (1968): 336-353.

968. Atkins, A. "The Moderate Optimism of Saul Bellow's *Herzog*."
      Person, 50 (1969) : 117-129.

969. Barth, J. R., ed. *Religious Perspectives in Faulkner's Fiction:
      Yoknapatawpha and Beyond*. Notre Dame, Ind.: University of
      Notre Dame Press, 1972.

970. Beisly, P. "The Function of Criticism and Tragedy," *NewBl*, 53
      (1972) : 367-379. Reply, Stein, W. "Criticism and Tragedy,"
      NewBl, 53 (1972) : 416-423.

971. Brunauer, D. H. "Creative Faith in Wilder's *The Eighth Day*,"
      Renascence, 25, i (1972) : 46-56.

972. Burke, K. *Language as Symbolic Action: Essays on Life, Litera-
      ture and Method*. University of California Press, 1966.

973. Burke, K. *Philosophy of Literary Form: Studies in Symbolic Ac-
      tion*. 2nd ed. Baton Rouge: LSU Press, 1967.

974. Burke, K. *The Rhetoric of Religion; Studies in Logology*. Boston:
      Beacon Press, 1961.

975. Campbell, J. *The Hero With A Thousand Faces*. New York:
      Pantheon Books, 1949.

976. Carr, J. "An Interview with Walker Percy," *GeorR*, 25 (1971) :
      317-332.

977. Cassirer, E. *Language and Myth*. Tr. by S. Langer. New York:
      Dover Publications, 1946. [Originally published 1925.]

978. Cassirer, E. *The Philosophy of Symbolic Forms*. 3 vols. See esp.
      vol. I, Language; vol. II, Mythical Thought. Tr. by R. Man-
      heim. New Haven: Yale University Press, 1953 (vol. I); 1955
      (vol. II).

979. Castelli, J. "Catch-22 and the New Hero," *CathW*, 211 (August
      1970) : 199-202.

980. Detweiler, R. *Commentary on Iris Murdoch's The Unicorn*. [L.
      Belford, ed., Religious Dimensions in Literature Series.] New
      York: Seabury, 1969.

981. Douglas, E. *Commentary on Walker Percy's The Last Gentleman*.
      [L. Belford, ed., Religious Dimensions in Literature Series.]
      New York: Seabury, 1969.

982. Fairman, M. *Biblical Patterns in Modern Literature*. Lakewood,
      Ohio: Dillon/Liederbach, Inc., 1972.

983. Golden, R. E. "Mass Man and Modernism: Violence in Pynchon's
      V.," *Crit*, 14, ii (1972) : 5-17.

984. Goldstein, B. & S. "Bunnies and Cobras: Zen Enlightenment in Salinger," *Discourse*, 13 (Winter 1970): 98-106.

985. Gordon, D. J. "The Tale and the Artist," *YR*, 62 (1973): 168-185.

986. Harris, C. B. *Contemporary American Novelists of the Absurd.* New Haven: College and University Press, 1972.

987. Hart, R. *Unfinished Man and the Imagination; Toward an Ontology and a Rhetoric of Revelation.* New York: Herder & Herder, c. 1968.

988. Hassan, I. *Contemporary American Literature 1945-1972: An Introduction.* New York: Ungar, 1973.

989. Jarrett-Kerr, M. *William Faulkner.* Contemporary Writers in Christian Perspective Series. New York: Eerdmanns, 1970.

990. Kaelin, E. F. *An Existentialist Aesthetic: The Theories of Sartre and Merleau-Ponty.* Madison: University of Wisconsin Press, 1962.

991. Killinger, J. *The Fragile Presence; Transcendence in Modern Literature.* Philadelphia, Penna.: Fortress Press, 1973.

992. Langer, S. K. *Feeling and Form: A Theory of Art Developed from Philosophy in a New Key.* London: Routledge & K. Paul, 1953.

993. Langer, S. K. *Problems of Art: Ten Philosophical Lectures.* New York: Scribner, 1957.

994. Livingston, J. C. *Commentary on William Golding's The Spire.* [L. Belford, ed., Religious Dimensions in Literature Series.] New York: Seabury, 1967.

995. Luschei, M. *The Sovereign Wayfarer: Walker Percy's Diagnosis of the Malaise.* Baton Rouge: Louisiana State University Press, 1972.

996. Lynch, W. F. *Christ and Prometheus; A New Image of the Secular.* Notre Dame: University of Notre Dame Press, 1972.

997. Merton, T. *Commentary on Albert Camus' The Plague.* [L. Belford, ed., Religious Dimensions in Literature Series.] New York: Seabury, n.d.

998. Montgomery, M. "In Defense of Flannery O'Connor's Dragon," *GeorR*, 25 (1971): 302-316.

999. Mueller, W. R. *Celebration of Life; Studies in Modern Fiction.* New York: Sheed & Ward, 1972.

1000. O'Flaherty, K. "François Mauriac, 1885-1970: An Effort at Assessment," *Studies,* 60 (1971): 33-42.

1001. Olderman, R. M. *Beyond the Waste Land: A Study of the American Novel in the Nineteen-Sixties.* New Haven and London: Yale Univ. Press, 1972.

1002. Ricoeur, P. *The Symbolism of Evil.* Tr. by E. Buchanan. New York: Harper & Row, 1967.

1003. Rovit, E. "On the Contemporary Apocalyptic Imagination," *ASch,* 37 (1968): 458-463.

1004. Sayers, D. L. *Christian Letters To A Post-Christian World.* Grand Rapids, Mich.: Wm. B. Eerdmans Publishing Co., 1969. See esp. "Man: The Creating Creature", pp. 69-129, and "Christian Imagination in a Post-Christian World", pp. 159-236.

1005. Sayers, D. L. *The Mind of the Maker.* New York: Meridian Books, 1956.

1006. Schroth, R. A. "Exorcising the Exorcist," *Commonweal,* 97, v (1972): 110-112. Reply by W. J. O'Malley, "An Exchange of Views: Exorcising the Exorcist," 97, xi (1972): 252-254. Rejoinder, Mr. Schroth, 254-255.

1007. Scott, N. A., Jr. " 'New Heav'ns, New Earth'—the Landscape of Contemporary Apocalypse," *JR,* 53 (1973): 1-35.

1008. Spanos, W. V. "Modern Literary Criticism and the Spatialization of Time," *JAAC,* 29 (1970): 87-104.

1009. Swanson, W. J. "Religious Implications in *The Confessions of Nat Turner,*" *CimR,* #12 (July 1970): 57-66.

1010. Utley, F. L., L. Z. Bloom, and A. Kinney, eds. *Bear, Man and God: Seven Approaches to Faulkner's "The Bear."* New York: Random House, 1964.

1011. Wilder, A. N. "The Rhetoric of Ancient and Modern Apocalyptic," *Interpretation,* 25 (1971): 436-453.

Appendix III

1012. Browning, P. M., Jr. "Flannery O'Connor and the Demonic," *MFS,* 19 (1973): 29-41.

1013. Coale, S. "The Quest for the Elusive Self: the Fiction of Jerzy Kosinski," *Crit,* 14 (1973): 25-37.

1014. Dorenkamp, J. H. "The Unity of *Morte D'Urban,*" *UDR,* 8 (1971): 29-34.

1015. Friedman, A. W. "Joyce Cary's Cubistic Morality," *ConL,* 14 (1973): 78-96.

1016. Frost, L. "The Drowning of American Adam: Hawkes' *The Beetle Leg,*" *Crit,* 14 (1973): 63-74.

1017. Gaston, P. "The Revelation of Walker Percy," *ColQ,* 20 (1972): 459-470.

1018. Gindin, J. "Megalotopia and the WASP Backlash: The Fiction of Mailer and Updike," *CentR,* 15 (1971): 38-52.

1019. Grant, P. "Tolkien: Archetype and Word," *CrCur,* 22 (1973): 365-380.

1020. Hamilton, K. *In Search of Contemporary Man.* Contemporary Writers in Christian Perspective Series. Grand Rapids, Mich.: Wm. B. Eerdmans, 1967.

1021. Hansen, A. J. "The Celebration of Solipsism: A New Trend in American Fiction," *MFS,* 19 (1973): 5-15.

1022. Harris, J. N. "One Critical Approach to Mr. Sammler's Planet," *TCL,* 18 (1972): 235-250.

1023. Pinsker, S. "Saul Bellow in the Classroom," *CE,* 34 (1973): 975-982.

1024. Saliers, D. E. "Faith and the Comic Eye: Religious Gleanings from Comic Vision in Some Recent Fiction," *ANQ,* 13 (1973): 259-276.

1025. Schaeffer, S. F. *"Bend Sinister* and the Novelist as Anthropomorphic Deity," *CentR,* 17 (1973): 115-151. [Nabokov]

1026. Schlueter, P. "Post-Modern Temper of Recent Literature: Nathan Scott on Art and Sacrament," *JR,* 53 (1973): 104-116.

1027. Stetler, C. "Purdy's *Malcolm:* Allegory of No Man," *Crit,* 14 (1973): 91-99.

1028. Vargo, E. P. "The Necessity of Myth in Updike's *The Centaur,*" *PMLA,* 88 (1973): 452-460.

1029. White, J. J. *Mythology in the Modern Novel: A Study of Prefigurative Techniques.* Princeton: Princeton University Press, 1971.

PRIMARY AND
SECONDARY AUTHOR INDEX

PRIMARY AND SECONDARY AUTHOR INDEX

SECONDARY AUTHORS

A

Abrams, M. H., 87, 88
Adams, H. B., 176
Allentuck, M., 642
Alter, R., 37, 190
Altieri, C. F., 963
Altizer, T. J. J., 964
Amstutz, J., 58
Anderson, D., 1
Antico, J., 103
Arnold, W. E., 220
Arseniev, N. S., 790
Asals, F., 525
Ashida, M. E., 104
Astro, R., 666
Atkins, A., 2, 593, 965, 968
Auden, W. H., 896
Auerbach, E., 735
Austin, A., 812, 813
Axthelm, P. M., 280
Ayo, N., 714

B

Babbage, S., 736
Backman, M., 472
Baird, Sister M. J., 584
Baker, C., 96, 473
Baldanza, F., 657
Balke, B. T., 623
Banks, A. C., 487
Barber, D. K., 688
Barnes, R. J., 281
Barr, D., 624
Barth, J. R., 373, 374, 737, 969
Bassan, M., 526
Bates, B. W., 602
Battenhouse, R. W., 814
Baumbach, J., 282, 498, 527
Bedell, G. C., 815, 816, 897
Beebe, H. K., 308
Beisly, P., 970
Bellow, S., 309
Berger, P., 322
Bergup, Sister B., 528
Bertrande, Sister, 529

Bethell, S. L., 816
Biles, J. I., 400
Birmingham, W., 428
Björk, L., 375
Blehl, V. F., 817
Bloom, E. A., 837
Bloom, L. Z., 1010
Bloom, R., 362, 818
Bloomfield, C., 83
Blotner, J., 376
Bode, C., 234
Bodtke, R., 710
Boies, J. J., 106
Boklund, G., 38
Bone, R., 601
Borowitz, E. B., 191
Boulger, J. D., 107
Boyd, A. S., 152
Boyd, G. N., 68
Boyle, R., 603
Bradbury, J. M., 283
Bradford, M. E., 474
Brawer, J., 363
Braybrooke, N., 108, 401, 402
Brée, G., 323, 508
Brittain, J. T., 908
Brockmann, C. B., 324
Broes, A. T., 403
Brooks, C., 227, 284, 377
Brown, A., 423
Brown, R. Mc., 3
Browning, P. M., Jr., 530, 531, 1012
Brumm, U., 43, 44, 169
Brunauer, D. H., 971
Bryant, J. H., 676
Bryant, R. H., 325
Bryer, J. R., 885
Buchen, I. H., 643, 644, 645
Buckley, V., 819, 820
Bufkin, E. C., 404
Bunting, J. J., Jr., 4
Burchard, R. C., 898
Burgess, A., 899
Burhans, C. S., Jr., 475
Burke, E. L., 326
Burke, J. J., 532

THE COMPILERS

THE COMPILERS

George Nolan Boyd holds the B. A. degree from Austin College, Sherman, Texas, and the master of divinity degree from Austin Presbyterian Theological Seminary. He earned the doctorate in theology from Union Theological Seminary in New York and also pursued graduate studies in Berne, Switzerland.

Dr. Boyd has taught at Colgate University and since 1969 at Trinity University. He has published articles in the areas of contemporary theology, religion and literature, and film criticism.

Lois A. Boyd received the bachelor of journalism degree from the University of Texas. She has worked in public relations with a television, radio, and film production unit, served as associate editor of a monthly publication, and done free-lance writing.